THE RUG MERCHANT OF CHAOS
AND OTHER PLAYS

THE RUG MERCHANT OF CHAOS
AND OTHER PLAYS

Ronald Ribman

Theatre Communications Group
1992

The Rug Merchants of Chaos and Other Plays is published by Theatre Communications Group, Inc., 355 Lexington Ave., New York, NY 10017.

TCG gratefully acknowledges public funds from the National Endowment for the Arts, the New York State Council on the Arts and the New York City Department of Cultural Affairs in addition to the generous support of the following foundations and corporations: Alcoa Foundation, Ameritech Foundation, ARCO Foundation, AT&T Foundation, Citibank N.A., Consolidated Edison Company of New York, Council of Literary Magazines and Presses, Nathan Cummings Foundation, Dayton Hudson Foundation, Exxon Corporation, Ford Foundation, GTE, James Irvine Foundation, Jerome Foundation, Management Consultants for the Arts, Andrew W. Mellon Foundation, Metropolitan Life Foundation, National Broadcasting Company, Pew Charitable Trusts, Philip Morris Companies Inc., Scherman Foundation, Shubert Foundation, L. J. Skaggs and Mary C. Skaggs Foundation, Lila Wallace-Reader's Digest Fund.

Ribman, Ronald.
The rug merchants of chaos, and other plays / Ronald Ribman.—1st ed.
Contents: Buck—Sweet table at the Richelieu—The rug merchants of chaos.
ISBN 1-55936-050-X (cloth)—ISBN 1-55936-049-6 (paper)
I. Title.
PS3568.I2R84 1992
812'.54—dc20 92-2568
CIP

Design and composition by G&H/SOHO, Ltd.

First Edition, June 1992

CONTENTS

BUCK

For the ladies and gentlemen of the Rockefeller Foundation whose encouragement and support over the years has greatly mattered.

Buck was first presented at the American Place Theatre in New York City, February 24, 1983, as a co-production by the American Place Theatre and Playwrights Horizons. Elinor Renfield directed. The set was designed by John Arnone, the lighting by Frances Aronson, the costumes by David C. Woolard and the sound by Paul Garrity. The cast was as follows:

Buck Halloran .... Alan Rosenberg
Charlie Corvanni .... Robert Silver
Fred Milly .... Morgan Freeman
Professor Pipe-in-the-Mouth/Frank .... Jack Davidson
Mr. Lollipop .... Bernie Passeltiner
Mr. Hawaiian Shirt .... Ted Sod
Joy Bonnard/Shirley .... Priscilla Lopez
Salesman .... Michael Lipton
Mr. Heegan .... Richard Leighton
Vendor .... Jimmy Smits
Woman with Turban .... Madeleine le Roux
Milton Berman/Derelict .... Bernie Passeltiner
Mr. Goglas/Ramon Luis de la Barca .... Ted Sod
Vincente/A Young Actor .... Jimmy Smits
Madame/A Middle-aged Actress .... Madeleine le Roux
Mr. Nathan .... Joseph Leon
Stagehands .... Mitchell Gossett, Nick Iacovino, Charles Kindl, Michael Linden, Kenneth Lodge, Richard Mandel, Michael O'Boyll, Jason O'Malley, David Sennett

CHARACTERS

BUCK HALLORAN
CHARLIE CORVANNI
FRED MILLY
PROFESSOR PIPE-IN-THE-MOUTH/FRANK
MR. LOLLIPOP
MR. HAWAIIAN SHIRT
JOY BONNARD/SHIRLEY
SALESMAN
MR. HEEGAN
VENDOR
WOMAN WITH TURBAN
MILTON BERMAN/DERELICT
MR. GOGLAS/RAMON LUIS ÇARPIO DE LA BARCA
VINCENTE/A YOUNG ACTOR
MADAM/A MIDDLE-AGED ACTRESS
MR. NATHAN
STAGEHANDS (nonspeaking)

TIME

Early 1980s.

PLACE

Act One
Scene 1: A cable TV studio.
Scene 2: A department store.
Scene 3: A bar.
Scene 4: The studio.

Act Two
The studio, the following week.

ACT ONE

Scene 1

A cable television studio. The studio is in the cavernous, windowless basement of an old building. Beyond stage left and stage right is a darkness, the end of which cannot be seen. Upstage left, several steps above the basement floor, is a large freight elevator. Downstage left on the basement floor is a large worktable with several chairs behind it. The worktable is littered with papers, ashtrays, pens, pencils, a Silex of coffee, cups, an open box of jelly donuts and a phone. Nearby can be seen a portable television camera resting on a tripod, and some television monitoring equipment on a stand. Upstage right, near the rear wall of the basement, is a movable platform used as a production set. The set, at the moment, is that of a rather rundown-looking apartment, the apartment suggested mostly by the few pieces of furniture in it: a small sofa; an end table with a half-finished sweater lying on top of it, knitting needles poking through; a linen-shaded floor lamp; a small liquor cabinet; a phony wooden fireplace. Because the platform has been turned around to face the upstage wall and is unlit, nothing can be seen of the apartment except the outside scrim walls. A number of television cables, feeding out of a downstage right outlet, run across the entire rim of the stage.

A cone of light illuminates Buck Halloran as he sits behind the worktable, staring blankly forward. Buck is a man in his middle to late thirties; his eyes are dark and tired. As the cone of light expands to reveal another man, Charlie Corvanni, seated behind the table, Buck shuts his eyes, pressing the tips of his fingers against them. Charlie, close in age to Buck, is intently interested, at the moment, in selecting a good jelly donut for himself. The one he has just bitten into has brought a sour expression to his face. He looks at the donut, sticks his tongue out in disgust, and then putting the donut aside, reaches into the box for a new one. The new one is as much a loser as the first, as far as Charlie is concerned. Charlie, in despair, lowers the second donut to the table. The cone of light continues to expand, illuminating the entire stage left side of the basement to the elevator.

CHARLIE: What kind of jelly donut did you get, Buck?

BUCK: I got a blueberry one, Charlie.

CHARLIE: Boy, they're the best ones, aren't they? They got the most powdered sugar on them and everything.

BUCK: That's right, Charlie.

CHARLIE: I mean even on the inside they're the best because they got whole pieces of berries, while the others just got jam or something.

BUCK: You better believe it, Charlie.

CHARLIE: Boy, this one I'm eating now tastes like it was filled with mushrooms or something.

Buck, his eyes still closed, has begun massaging his temples with his fingertips.

I don't know what it is with me. I always reach for the ones with the most powdered sugar on them because I know the ones with the most powdered sugar on them are the blueberry ones, but I always end up with the ones that taste like mushroom. (*Grabs another donut out of the box, bites into it, makes a sour face, and puts it down*) You always get the best. (*Pause*) I guess all I can do is keep trying, huh, Buck?

BUCK: That's right, Charlie. All you can do is keep trying.

Suddenly the elevator snaps into life with a shrill whine, its descent marked by a pulsing red lightbulb above the elevator door. Buck's eyes pop open. Charlie jumps to his feet, in his fright knocking over a stack of paper coffee cups. He scrambles about the floor, trying to collect them before whoever it is in the elevator arrives.

CHARLIE: Oh, shit . . . oh, shit.

The elevator door suddenly opens, an almost blinding white light pouring out. The object of their trepidation, Fred Milly, stands motionless in the elevator for a few moments. Milly is a large black man with an awesome-looking club foot. He is impeccably dressed in an expensive business suit, his fingers displaying several gold and diamond rings. Milly enjoys his joviality and his smile, though it is the all-too-evident unnerving smile of a cobra.

MILLY: How you boys doing?

CHARLIE (*As eager to please as a fawning dog*): Great, Mr. Milly. Just great. Can I get you a cup of coffee?

As Milly steps forward, the elevator door snaps shut behind him.

MILLY: I like what you do with your camera, Charlie. You do nice work.

CHARLIE: Thanks a lot, Mr. Milly. I appreciate that coming from you.

MILLY (*Beginning his awkward clubfooted descent down the three steps into the basement*): But you never call me Fred. I tell you to call me Fred, but you never call me Fred.

CHARLIE: Can I get you a cup of coffee, Fred?

MILLY: Sure. You get me a black cup of coffee. That's what I like . . . just black.

Milly laughs loudly at his own private joke as Charlie pours him a cup of coffee.

BUCK: I'll have these cost figures for you in a second, Fred.

MILLY: How come you don't call me Mr. Milly?

BUCK: Whatever you say, Mr. Milly.

MILLY: Sure. That's good. I like that, too. You call me Mr. Milly. Charlie calls me Fred. Everybody calls me something different.

Milly laughs loudly again as Charlie comes forward, the coffee in his outstretched hand.

How's your two little girls, Charlie?

CHARLIE: They ain't so little anymore, Fred. They're in Junior High School.

Charlie continues to hold the cup of coffee out to Milly, who makes no movement to take it.

MILLY: Junior High School, is that a fact?

CHARLIE: Yes, sir, that's right.

MILLY: Well, that's wonderful, Charlie. Just wonderful. All those wonderful Junior High School dances and basketball games to go to. Wonderful time in a young girl's life . . . especially if she's pretty. Your girls pretty, Charlie?

CHARLIE (*Lowering his arm*): They do okay in that department, Fred.

Milly finally holds out his hand to take the coffee, forcing Charlie to hold the cup out again.

MILLY: I bet they do.

Milly laughs again, nudging Charlie, as if the two of them were sharing some kind of private dirty joke. Charlie nervously joins in the laughter.

Pretty girls never have any trouble getting themselves all the dates they want, do they, Charlie? Phones ringing all the time, boys with hot pants sitting around outside in their cars, honking their horns, jiggling their hands around in their pockets, waiting to take them to all those wonderful Junior High School dances and basketball games. Show me a picture of them, Charlie.

Charlie, uncertain, hesitates for a moment, and then, slightly turning away from Milly, reaches into his back pocket for his wallet.

It's absolutely incredible what people try to hide away in their wallets and purses: old photos, torn ticket stubs, little pieces of lint and cellophane, tinfoil prophylactics waiting so long to get used they make ringworms in the leather. (*He takes the photo Charlie has produced and looks at it*) Pretty, Charlie, pretty. (*Holding the picture up and rhapsodizing into a few lines of Sapphic verse*)

> "Like the sweet apple ripening atop the topmost bough,
> Atop the topmost limb, which the pluckers forgot—
> Forgot it not, nay, but got it not!
> For none could get it till now."

(*Handing Charlie back his photo*) Don't let the boys get them too soon, Charlie.

Charlie puts the photo away and sits down at the worktable.

The boys always want to pluck our sweet apples too soon.

CHARLIE: Don't worry, Fred, I can always hear a plucker coming a mile away.

For a moment a small smile plays on Milly's face and then he lifts up his club foot and crashes it down on the table.

MILLY: Now I remember when I was back in Junior High School. Tried out for the baseball team, but I couldn't make it out of the locker room in time. Tried out for the football team, but I couldn't get my foot through the leggings in time. Tried out for the track team, but I accidently crushed another runner's foot in the relay. I guess the only thing I got to on time was the graduation prom. That was a wonderful night, so wonderful. Dancing and dancing under the Alabama stars, whirling down the white colonnades with all those pretty Alabama girls in their perfumed corsages and crinoline dresses, sneaking in a little kiss from their pouty little red mouths, crushing their starchy skirts into my genitals till they exploded like jellied gasoline. (*Laughing heartily at his memories*)

CHARLIE: Boy, you sure can't buy memories like that. (*Pause*) Why don't you sit down, Fred? Take a load off your foot.

The smile on Milly's face drains away as he slowly draws his club foot off the table. Opening a folder lying on the table in front of Charlie, Milly suddenly jabs his finger into the middle of one of the pages.

MILLY: What's this thing for twenty-four dollars?

CHARLIE: A vibrator I had to buy for the show.

MILLY: Twenty-four dollars?

CHARLIE: That's what it cost.

MILLY: Twenty-four dollars?

CHARLIE: We needed a good sound to pick up on the audio equipment!

MILLY (*Picking up a pencil and applying greater and greater pressure against it as his voice rises in intensity*): Twenty-four dollars!

CHARLIE (*Turning to Buck for help*): Isn't that right, Buck? We needed a good sound to pick up on the audio equipment?

MILLY: Twenty-four dollars!

CHARLIE: We followed the police reports! It was the same vibrator the girl was using when she was killed! Isn't that right, Buck? Buck!

MILLY: Twenty-four dollars! Twenty-four dollars!

The pencil snaps in Milly's hand as Charlie cracks under the strain and blurts out his confession.

CHARLIE: Seventeen dollars! I only paid seventeen dollars, Fred.

MILLY: Why don't you call me Mr. Milly, Charlie? (*Becoming gently paternalistic*) Oh, Charlie, what a world we live in. Greed, avarice, corruption, nobody satisfied with what they got, always wanting more. If I could give you one word of advice, one word that would sum up everything I've learned about life, it would be this—be sincere. (*Placing his club foot on top of Charlie's toes and gradually increasing the pressure*) How does that song go? "I'd like to teach the world to sing in perfect harmony. I'd like to buy the world a Coke and keep it company. That's the real thing."

While Milly's foot presses down on Charlie's toes in time to the song, Charlie does everything he can to withstand the crushing pain, including a kind of silent singalong with Milly.

Well, Charlie, that's what sincerity is—the real thing.

CHARLIE: I've been as sincere with you as you've been with me, Fred! (*The attempt to continue calling Milly by his first name fails as the pain becomes unbearable. He screams out in agony*) Mr. Milly! Mr. Milly!

MILLY (*Lifting his club foot from Charlie's toes in total victory, and moving over to Buck*): And you, Buck? Have you been as sincere with me as I've been with you?

BUCK: Sure, Mr. Milly.

MILLY: Just call me Fred, Buck. (*Sitting down next to Buck*) I'm glad because I want you to know I never miss a chance telling the big boys upstairs what a hell of a job you're doing down here with your murder reenactments, and how I think you're ready to move up to major corporate responsibility. You believe me, Buck? You believe I'm doing these things for you?

BUCK: Sure, Fred.

MILLY: That's fine, Buck. Only I can't push you too hard. I push you too hard there's a chance they may cool off on you. So what I'm doing now, Buck, is working on them one at a time. I'm casting the old fishing plug out for Mr. Nathan right now. It may take a couple of months, maybe even a year, but once he snaps at your bait and I get the hook set deep in his mouth, I can reel him in and start trolling for Mr. Jacobs and Mr. Stein. Once we gaff 'em good, Buck, we can start dragging your meat in front of the big one—Mr. St. George. We get his salivary glands going for you, Buck, we get him thrashing and drooling in the water over your chitterlings, there ain't nothing gonna keep you outta that board room.

BUCK: Sure, Fred.

MILLY: Unless of course they was to get it in their head you've been dragging your feet on the Joy Bonnard murder reenactment . . . get it in their head you got problems taping the killing of that department-store perfume-counter whore by the college professor. . . . Why then who knows what could happen . . . they get something like that in their head.

BUCK: Sure, Fred.

MILLY (*Sliding back his chair and standing up*): Well, I gotta get on my horse. I can't tell you how much your faith in me means, Buck, and how much I look forward to these little visits with you in the basement.

As Milly heads toward the elevator, Buck and Charlie begin visibly breathing with relief. Charlie has just stuffed a new jelly donut in his mouth as Milly pauses for a moment on the steps.

Oh, by the way . . .

The donut literally drops out of Charlie's mouth as both he and Buck turn simultaneously to look at Milly.

I guess you heard about the funny thing that happened to Mr. Nathan when he came to work this morning. (*He presses the elevator button and the door opens, flooding everything in front of it with its harsh white light*) It seems he saw an old crone of a woman setting up an applecart in the lobby. It threw him into a panic. He told Mr. Jacobs, and Mr. Jacobs told Mr. Stein, and Mr. Stein told Mr. St. George. The rumor now is that if she's still there tomorrow her applecart may trigger a depression in the entire industry. We may have to expect some layoffs from the bottom of the building up. (*Stepping into the elevator*) Well, trust me, Buck. Trust me. Nobody's in here more solid than you are.

Milly presses the button to shut the elevator door. The last sound we hear before the door shuts and the elevator begins its noisy ascent is Milly's final laugh. Milly has no sooner exited than the phone on the worktable begins to ring. It rings and rings, both men obviously afraid to pick it up. Buck finally reaches for it.

BUCK: News reenactments. Buck Halloran speaking. (*Pause*) Good morning, Mr. Nathan. How are you this—

Buck never has a chance to finish, and the artificial smile he has glued to his face disintegrates in an instant. When he speaks now, his voice is a blur of fear. The stage lights begin contracting, until by the end of his conversation Buck is left standing alone in a pool of light.

I never said anything like that to Mr. Milly, so I don't know why Mr. Milly would say anything like that to you, or how Mr. Milly could be standing in your office on the top floor right now when the elevator door just shut on Mr. Milly and the elevator is still rising! (*Pause*) I never never never said anything about being unhappy with my job and feeling that the expense of my divorce gave me the right to mark up the price of a vibrator to supplement my income. (*Pause*) I am not accusing Mr. Milly of being insincere! I realize his level of sincerity is higher than my own since he occupies a higher position of trust than I do, but I know that I am being sincere when I tell you that I am happy happy happy with my job and I would never do anything to jeopardize it by dragging my feet on the Joy Bonnard murder reenactment, or phonying up the expense sheet on the vibrator! (*Caller has hung up*) Mr. Nathan? (*Screaming into the phone*) Mr. Nathan!

Buck slams the phone down, and for a moment stands there panicked and struggling to catch his breath. The lights on the upstage production set begin to come up, allowing us to see through the scrim walls into the apartment. The light comes from three sources: the yellow bulb of the floor lamp, the red glow of the phony logs "burning" in the phony fireplace, and a pair of sconces set up over the mantle. There are three men and a young woman (Joy Bonnard) in the apartment. The youngest man (Mr. Hawaiian Shirt), his hair slick and greasy, wears his loud shirt over his pants; the middle-aged man (Professor Pipe-in-the-Mouth/Frank), distinguished-looking as he sucks on his pipe, is dressed only in his briefs; the old man (Mr. Lollipop), sucking a lollipop, is in an undershirt, his baggy pants held up by suspenders. As Joy, dressed in a flowing white dressing gown, moves among them, the men reach out, grabbing at her, assaulting her. At the first sound, Buck has whirled around to face the nightmarish events taking place in the apartment behind the scrim.

PROFESSOR PIPE-IN-THE-MOUTH/FRANK: Come on over here, you witless bimbo! I want you to lie down next to me on the couch! I want you to pretend you've got something to offer a man besides your body!

MR. LOLLIPOP: Could we pretend we're sixteen years old and we live in a little house in the forest and the snow is coming down?

MR. HAWAIIAN SHIRT: Lick me all over! I wanna go around the world! Get off your goddam high horse, Miss Joy Bonnard, and gimme what I want!

MR. LOLLIPOP: I want you to put on a garter belt and a pair of black stockings! That's the only thing that gets me up anymore!

PROFESSOR PIPE-IN-THE-MOUTH/FRANK: You know what it's like for me facing four hundred morons in a lecture hall and trying to teach them something about Kierkegaard? Listen to me! They're eating me alive! They're sucking out my marrow and eating me alive!

MR. LOLLIPOP: I want to pretend with you! Joy? Joy!

MR. HAWAIIAN SHIRT: I want you to get down on the floor! I want you to spread your legs because I'm gonna do whatever I wanna do with you!

PROFESSOR PIPE-IN-THE-MOUTH/FRANK: You dumb whore! You moronic slut! You tell me what the salesgirl behind the department-store perfume counter thinks anybody would be interested in hearing her talk about!

The scrim door to the apartment swings open and Joy stands in the doorway confronting Buck. There is a weariness to her face as she stares at him, as if he might be just another exploiter. He takes several steps towards her and then stops as the hands of the men behind her wind about her face and body like the slow-moving tentacles of an octopus. Buck whirls forward, pressing the fingers of his hands against his skull as behind him Joy is slowly drawn back into the apartment. Lights dim and out.

Scene 2

A department store. Sound of store chimes in the dark followed by a soft sensual female voice over the loudspeaker.

VOICE: Discover the fragrance of summer. Come meet Joy and sample the woodland scents of her summer collection: the crush of sweet grass on the forest floor, violets and sweet musk roses, woodbine and eglantine. Echoes of a time when all the world was young, and gentle knights with sword and lance took up the sacred quest to slay the dragon and right the wrong. Come to Joy now and let her cast your fragrance future with her new Lady Guinevere collection. With every purchase you'll receive a lovely lead-crystal spray dispenser for just twelve fifty. It's happening now at La Parfumerie. Main floor. Fifth Avenue exit.

The lights come up first on the well-dressed salesman standing behind his counter in the sporting goods department. The light emanating up from the counter casts an odd, almost devilish, shine on the salesman's smiling face. The counter light now fades away as the general lighting in the department store comes up. Buck stands some yards away from the salesman. Buck has a hunting arrow in his hand, and stares down at it, totally absorbed. The salesman watches him for some moments before speaking.

SALESMAN: If you're going to hunt large game, you couldn't pick a better arrow.

BUCK (*Almost as if coming out of a trance*): I . . . I was on my way to the perfume counter.

SALESMAN: The perfume counter's over there. (*Gesturing stage left*) You've been standing here with that arrow for quite some time.

BUCK: Have I? I was thinking about something. There was a girl who worked at the perfume counter . . . Joy Bonnard. Did you know her?

SALESMAN: Afraid not.

BUCK: She got murdered a while back. (*Looking down at the arrow again*)

SALESMAN: It *is* a beautiful instrument, isn't it?

BUCK: Yes.

SALESMAN (*Walking over to Buck*): Perfectly balanced, true in flight . . . one of the last few really beautiful things left in this world a man can rely on.

BUCK: It's not for target work, is it?

SALESMAN: No. It's for killing . . . just killing.

BUCK: Yes. You can see that just by looking at it. Does it have a name . . . if you were to ask for it . . . by name?

SALESMAN: It's a Rumsford razor point on a twenty-six-inch flexible aluminum shaft. It features a double blood groove and moisture-resistant New England turkey fletching.

BUCK: Fletching?

SALESMAN: Feathers.

BUCK: You could really kill something with this.

SALESMAN: Oh, yes. You could kill just about anything you wanted to with that.

BUCK: Yeah. I would like to kill something.

SALESMAN: Something specific in mind?

BUCK: I don't know. What would you suggest?

SALESMAN: Deer are nice. Wild boar, antelope.

BUCK: Something bigger, stronger.

SALESMAN: Elk, moose?

BUCK: Stronger, furrier. Something that would make a good rug. What's doing in the way of buffalo?

SALESMAN: African?

BUCK: American.

SALESMAN: The American buffalo is on the restricted game list. They're an endangered species, protected by law.

BUCK: Just suppose I found a way to get around all that legalistic crap and wanted to kill one of them. I could do it with this. Right?

SALESMAN: Right.

BUCK: One stick and it's over with. Hit the skull and the eyes pop out. Hit the lung and a thousand legal injunctions collapse in a bag of wind.

SALESMAN: Over the foreleg into the heart. That's actually the best place to stick it for a good kill.

BUCK: That's the kind of information I need.

SALESMAN: Ever hunt before?

BUCK: No. Does it count against me?

SALESMAN: Not if the desire is there.

BUCK: I've wanted to kill something for a long time. How does it actually do it? Sever an artery? And then these little things . . .

SALESMAN: The blood grooves.

BUCK: They would help, too, huh?

SALESMAN: Oh, yes.

BUCK: Sure. They would prevent the blood from clotting. The body would naturally want to clot, protect itself, but they would prevent it from doing that. They would just make sure the blood kept pouring out.

SALESMAN: You have a good instinct for the kill.

BUCK: You know it.

SALESMAN: Men with a good instinct for the kill always make the best hunters.

BUCK: How long does it take to kill something with this?

SALESMAN: A few minutes.

BUCK: From the time I first stick it into the rug, or the time it rolls over on the ground.

SALESMAN: The time it rolls over on the ground.

BUCK: And then what, while I'm waiting for it to die? Smoke a cigarette? Stare at the sky? Clean the day's filth from the ends of my fingernails?

SALESMAN: Do whatever you want, or nothing. The hunter's only responsibility is a clean kill.

BUCK: But what do I do if it isn't a clean kill? If the rug doesn't die right away? If it just lies there on the ground writhing in agony, blood gushing out of its side? What do I do then? Cut its throat? Step forward with some penknife, kitchen knife . . . ?

SALESMAN: No problem, sir. Our hunting department recommends the five-inch MacFadden dressing knife with bone handle, safety lock, and a high-tempered carbon steel blade.

BUCK (*Growing increasingly anguished*): And if it starts screaming when I slash its neck with the five-inch MacFadden! Bellowing in pain as the blade twists into the windpipe, severing cartilage and arteries, veins . . . severing it from air and voice, the ability to breathe and cry, everything that made it what it was, a hundred million years that made it what it was pouring out through flayed skin: blood, serum, mucus, bile . . .

SALESMAN: There's no need to go through that mess, sir. Many of our hunters prefer to have their game dressed at any one of a number of recommended butcher shops. I can give you a list of dressers that have served our clientele for many years. Six or a dozen, sir?

BUCK: What?

SALESMAN: Will that be six or a dozen, sir? The arrows are three ninety-eight each, twelve for forty-two dollars. You save the price of almost two arrows if you buy twelve.

BUCK: No. I don't want that many. I was just *looking* at this one. (*He hands the arrow to the salesman)*

SALESMAN: You can't count on getting a perfectly placed shot with one arrow.

BUCK: I was just passing by. I was just thinking.

Backing away from the salesman, Buck almost knocks into a floor display consisting of several Cub Scout mannequins gathered around a campfire in the forest. A number of toy archery sets are stacked up within the display.

SALESMAN (*Approaching Buck*): All right, sir. Just one it is then. Every sport has to have a beginning. I'm sure as soon as you use the Rumsford, you'll be back for more. That's the way it is with so many of our clients. One toe in the water at a time, and then they can't get enough. Will that be cash or charge?

Circling around the display as the salesman watches him, Buck seems visibly distressed.

BUCK: I don't have a charge card here, anymore. My wife used to.

SALESMAN: Might your wife be interested in hunting, too? We have a large selection of—

BUCK: My wife and I are divorced.

SALESMAN: Oh, that's too bad. Were there little ones?

BUCK: I had a little boy. I don't see him very much anymore.

SALESMAN: Oh, that's too bad. Divorce is always hardest on the fathers.

BUCK (*Suddenly picking up one of the toy archery sets*): What's the story on this? This thing's got a price tag on it for four ninety-eight.

SALESMAN: That's right.

BUCK: What's it on sale, or what?

SALESMAN: No, that's the regular price.

BUCK: How can it be the regular price? You're charging me three ninety-eight for one lousy arrow, and this whole outfit here is only a buck more? For a buck more, I get three arrows, a bow, a three-colored target, and an entire Indian headdress with pigeon feathers? That doesn't make any sense.

SALESMAN: Of course it does, sir. This is a real arrow. That's just a toy.

BUCK (*Walking away from the salesman, back to the counter*): Keep that arrow. I'm taking this. I'm not paying four dollars for one arrow when I can buy the whole ball of wax for a buck more!

SALESMAN: Look at those little arrows! They're fourteen-inch little arrows with rubber tips! (*Walking back to the counter*) You can't kill anything with them.

BUCK: You'd be surprised what you can do with suction tips. Once one of these babies sticks, it sticks!

SALESMAN: You can't hunt with that!

BUCK: Why? You think the animal's gonna know how much I spent on the equipment?

SALESMAN: But that's not the point, is it, sir? That's really not the point at all.

BUCK: Just give me this one.

SALESMAN (*Staring at Buck for some moments before he speaks*): Five forty with tax.

BUCK (*Putting some bills on the counter*): Keep the change. (*Starts to exit stage right, the toy archery set under his arm*)

SALESMAN: The perfume counter's the other way, bwana.

Buck changes his direction, backing away from the salesman, before turning and hastening off stage left.

(*Calling after Buck*) Catch you next time, bwana, when you're ready for the real thing.

The salesman drops the arrow back into the display case alongside the counter, and then spotting a new customer, leans forward with his hands on the counter and a fresh smile on his face. Lights dim and out. In the dark we hear a pop love ballad from the 1950s being sung. The music segues into the next scene.

Scene 3

A bar. The bar consists of a counter with a number of stools around it, a blue glass mirror behind the liquor bottles, and, inscribed above the mirror in stained glass letters, the names of the owners, "Boyle and Heegan." Downstage right is a small table with a couple of chairs.

Two customers are at the bar: one is a woman in a cheap-looking gaudy dress and a turban (Woman with Turban), the other a man with several layers of sweaters and a white apron, a vendor of some sort. As the bartender, Heegan, pours Buck a drink at the table, the music fades out.

HEEGAN: So I says to your Professor Pipe-in-the-Mouth, "No, it ain't July, it's December. Right around New Year's. That's when all the jerkos make their move." I tell him about this particular jerko who comes in here to rob the place around Christmas time. The jerko's doing his Christmas shopping, right? Right outta my cash register. Only he ain't even got a real gun. It's a plastic Luger he got outta Woolworth. I see what it is right away, but I don't let on, see? I give him the money and then as he's walking out the door I ease out my thirty-eight Colt Diamondback and I give him three quick ones right in the back. Bam, bam, bam! Enough to kill a water buffalo, right? Only the jerko son-of-a-bitch don't go down. He turns around as nice as you please like someone just tapped him on the shoulder, aims the plastic Luger right at my head and pulls the trigger. Piss, piss, piss—water comin' outta it, right? So I let him have two more in the gut. Pieces of his belt buckle flying up in the air, but he still ain't down.

VENDOR: How about somebody else putting in some change in the jukebox?

HEEGAN (*Ignoring the vendor*): He's hopping out the door, bleeding like a stuck pig, but still moving. By the time I catch up with him he's twenty yards down the street, sitting on a garbage can. I'm about to administer the coup de grace when he pitches over. "You understand what I'm gettin' at?," I says to your Professor Pipe-in-the-Mouth. "The thirty-eight ain't worth a shit! It ain't got no stopping power. You're gonna defend yourself, you gotta get something with real knockdown power, something you give them one shot and they're blown away." You wanna see what I'm packing now? (*Starts to open his jacket to expose a gun in a shoulder holster*)

VENDOR: How about somebody else coming up with some change?

HEEGAN: How about shutting your mouth?

VENDOR: You got no call saying that to me. I'm the only one feeding that machine. I just want somebody else—

HEEGAN: You wanna feed the machine, feed it! Don't tell anybody else what to do with their money! (*To Buck*) The less money they got, the bigger their mouth.

VENDOR: I wasn't telling anybody anything!

HEEGAN (*Opening his jacket again*): This is what I'm packing now.

WOMAN WITH TURBAN: I want a Chivas Regal on the rocks.

HEEGAN: We don't serve Chivas Regal here, lady. We serve bar whiskey and beer.

WOMAN WITH TURBAN: How about a frozen daiquiri? You got a frozen daiquiri?

HEEGAN: Do me a favor, lady. When you're finished with your beer, go back uptown to Maxwell's Plum or wherever it is you usually do your drinking.

WOMAN WITH TURBAN: What's the matter? You don't think I'm properly attired for this place? The man on 14th Street who sold me this dress said it was sleazy enough to get me in anywhere.

HEEGAN (*Taking the gun out and showing it to Buck*): This is what I'm packing now. You know what this is?

WOMAN WITH TURBAN: Your wee-wee.

HEEGAN (*Ignoring the remark*): This is the most powerful handgun in the world. Forty-four caliber magnum. The heaviest load in the world. Five times the juice of the thirty-eight. This baby drops one load they're gonna have to pick up your spine with a vacuum cleaner.

WOMAN WITH TURBAN: When you're finished showing off your wee-wee, you can get me a piña colada.

HEEGAN (*Still ignoring the woman, pulling a bullet out of the chamber to show Buck*): You see what I've done to this bullet? I've filed it down into a dum-dum. Every last bullet in this gun is a dum-dum.

WOMAN WITH TURBAN: Every last cell in your brain is a dum-dum.

HEEGAN: Listen, lady, why don't you just take a walk outta here? I'm trying to talk to this man. You know who this man is? This man's an important television producer. I'm trying to appraise him of a situation that happened here pertaining to a murder.

WOMAN WITH TURBAN: No shit!

HEEGAN: Look, lady, your beer's on the house. Just finish it up and take a walk outta here.

WOMAN WITH TURBAN: I'm waiting for my chauffeur.

BUCK (*To Heegan*): What else can you tell me about the professor?

HEEGAN: Not a hell of a lot more than I told your friend when he was in. He looked like a normal guy, you know, with a business suit. The only thing was he kept talking about some guy named Kierka something, and how he was going to be delivering a lecture on this guy, and the lecture had to be real good or they were going to eat him alive. I mean he was really concerned about that, like they were really going to eat him up.

WOMAN WITH TURBAN: You don't think I have a chauffeur? You imagine anyone using your facilities must be reduced to the same poverty of intellect and circumstances as yourself? Has it ever occurred to you that I may for reasons of my own prefer going around this way? Too much lipstick, too much face powder, a hideous dress of indisputable bad taste!

BUCK: What about the girl? Joy Bonnard.

HEEGAN: Yeah, she was different. She was a real sweetheart. I think she had a kid, but the kid died. You wanna find out about that you can ask them over in the department store across the street. She worked there in the perfume section.

BUCK: Yeah, I know. I already spoke to them. Go on.

HEEGAN: There's not much more I can tell ya. She'd come in three, four times a week, drink a couple of beers by herself, go on home. Always give you a smile on the way in, ask how you were, thank you whenever you brought over a drink. I guess she was kind of special now that I think about it. She kind of lit up the place. You could talk to her and she really listened. I just wish somewhere along the line I had said something to her about how nice she was.

VENDOR (*Flapping his apron up and down like a woman's skirt*): Hey, Heegan, you got a beer on the house for me, too?

HEEGAN (*To Buck*): I just wish I knew what that pipe-smoking son-of-a-bitch was going to do to her. I woulda blown his fucking head off! Go figure it—a college professor, right? The elite! What the hell you got left when they start doing things like that?

BUCK: She pick up a lot of guys in here?

HEEGAN: Hey, look, she's dead. What's the point in it?

BUCK: I just wanna know.

HEEGAN: Yeah, all right, sometimes. Like with Professor Pipe-in-the-Mouth. He was sitting in here when she came in. He went over, bought her a couple of drinks, and left with her. She was easy that way, I guess.

BUCK: She take money?

HEEGAN: Why? Is that what he said to the police?

BUCK: Yeah. He said she came at him with a knitting needle when he wouldn't pay.

HEEGAN: Yeah, well he's a fucking liar, isn't he?

BUCK: How do you know?

HEEGAN: Because I knew her! You knew her you wouldn't even ask things like that! She was no hooker. She was just a lonely kid who came in here for a few beers, and if she found someone to pass the night with, what the hell's the difference? It's no fun being alone, and I never heard no complaints from anybody who walked outta here with her.

BUCK (*Downing what's left of his drink and tossing some bills on the table as he starts to exit*): Appreciate your help, Mr. Heegan.

HEEGAN: Mr. Halloran?

Buck turns to look at him.

You ain't gonna fuck her, too, are you?

For a moment Heegan and Buck look at each other, and then Buck turns and exits. Heegan stands motionless for a few sec-

onds and then turns and angrily points a finger directly downstage.

Hey, you! That ain't no public toilet! You don't drink in here, you don't piss in here! Get out!

Lights dim and out.

Scene 4

The studio. The reenactment production set of Joy Bonnard's apartment has been brought downstage and turned around to face the audience.

In the dark we hear the sound of footsteps coming down a hall, laughter, and then the door to Joy's apartment opens and the sconce lights over the fireplace mantle come on. Joy enters, followed by Professor-Pipe-in-the-Mouth/Frank. He is well dressed in an overcoat and muffler. It has been snowing out and both are covered with melting flakes.

JOY (*Waving her hand around the apartment, her voice mixed with embarrassment and an attempt at lightheartedness*): Well, this is it.

Frank watches her move about swiftly, doing a last bit of straightening up: sofa pillows plumped, a dress gathered up, the floor lamp turned on, the phony flame in the phony fireplace set revolving.

I'm really sorry the apartment is in such a state. You'll have to excuse it. I wasn't expecting any visitors. (*Going over to him*) Let me take your coat. It's soaked through. (*Helping him off with his coat*) I hate it when it turns sleety that way. It soaks through everything. (*Holding his coat*) I'll hang it up in the bathroom. I'll be right back. Please make yourself at home.

Joy exits through a beaded archway on the stage-right side of the reenactment set, the archway presumably leading to her bedroom and bathroom. Frank stares about the room, examining the bric-a-brac and the dust.

FRANK (*Calling out as he lights his pipe*): How long have you lived here, Joy?

JOY (*Offstage*): Three years. I used to have a much nicer apartment on 23rd Street, but my girlfriend got married and the rent was too much. (*Returning to the room. The dress Joy has been wearing under her coat is tight, cheap, and provocative. It matches her manner, now*) What would you like to drink, Frank?

FRANK: Nothing for me. I think I just about had my limit at the bar. I'm feeling kind of woozy.

JOY: Oh, come on, don't be a spoilsport. What'll it be? I've got scotch, wine, brandy . . . whatever you like.

FRANK: I really shouldn't. I've got to deliver a paper tomorrow at the Modern Language Association meeting, and I haven't finished working on it yet.

JOY (*Waving the bottle*): One little drinky?

FRANK: Okay. Just one and then I gotta get going. I really do.

JOY: Sure. Just one. (*Pouring out two drinks and handing one to him*) Well, here's to . . . whatever.

They both take a swallow. Joy sits down on the couch and looks at Frank provocatively.

FRANK (*Uneasy*): I just wanted to make sure you got home safely, Joy. It's not much of a neighborhood out there.

JOY: Why don't you sit down beside me on the couch, Frank?

FRANK: All right.

JOY (*Moving over toward him on the couch*): This is much better, isn't it? (*Touching his face*) You have a nice face.

FRANK (*Grown visibly nervous*): I usually take my wife and kids into New York when I come, but our youngest came down with the flu, so I had to make the trip alone this time.

JOY (*Seductively continuing to touch him*): That's too bad.

FRANK: Yes.

JOY: Such warm-looking eyes. (*Running her fingers over his lips*) Sensitive mouth. (*Starting to unbutton his shirt*) All these buttons. So many buttons. I'm going to show you a very good time, Frank. I think we're going to have a very good time together.

FRANK: Joy, I think you misunderstood why I came up here. I really didn't intend—

JOY (*Placing her finger over his lips to silence him*): Do you like to dance, Frank?

FRANK: Sure.

JOY: Why don't you finish your drink, and I'll put on some music.

FRANK: I don't think I ought to drink anymore. I feel a little dizzy.

JOY: Oh, come on. One more little drink won't hurt anything. (*Lifting his glass to his mouth*) Bottoms up.

Frank finishes his drink. Joy walks over to the radio, a visible sway to her hips, and turns it on. She stands by the radio, arms out, fingers gesturing for him to join her. The music is slow, romantic, and her body moves provocatively to it. For some long moments Frank watches the lewd grinding of her hips, and then he gets to his feet. He is slightly unsteady, apparently due to the influence of alcohol. They begin to dance, her arms around his neck.

This is nice, isn't it?

FRANK: Yes.

JOY: You really should learn to relax. Your body is tense all over.

FRANK: I'm just not used to drinking. I feel so damn dizzy.

JOY (*Wetting her lips with her tongue*): Don't you like me?

FRANK: I can't do this. I can't. I've got a wife, kids . . .

JOY (*Overtly pressing her body into his groin as they dance*): But it feels so good, doesn't it?

FRANK: Yes.

JOY: You don't really want me to stop, do you, Frank? Should I stop?

She continues to grind her pelvis against him. Frank's breathing has become audible as the passion of the moment overcomes him.

I'll stop if you want me to, Frank. (*Sliding her body up and down against him*) I'm going to make you feel good all over, Frank. I want to show you the best time you ever had. You want that, don't you, Frank? Every man wants a good time.

As Frank holds her around the waist, Joy leans slightly back and unbuttons the front of her dress, pulling it back to partially expose her breasts. She places her hands under her breasts, cupping and squeezing them. Frank tries to draw her close to him, kiss her, but she starts to slightly resist, laughing.

I want it too, Frank. I want it as much as you do, but we have to settle the money thing. We have to get the money thing out of the way so we don't have to think about it.

Suddenly from the darkness, Buck yells out.

BUCK: Hold it! Hold it! (*Striding toward the reenactment set, waving his arms, shouting*) Gimme the lights! Just cut it! Cut everything!

The lights for the entire stage come on. The two actors playing the parts of Joy and Frank stand motionless, perplexed, on the set. Charlie hastens toward Buck.

CHARLIE: What the hell's the matter now!

BUCK: What the hell isn't the matter now! It's wrong! It's bullshit, and it's all wrong!

CHARLIE: What's wrong?

BUCK (*Stepping onto the reenactment set*): The fucking yellow lamp-light! What does she live in? An apartment in the East Village or a Chinese brothel? And that goddamn dress! The woman spent the day working in a department store! You think she waited on customers in a department store looking like that?

CHARLIE: Who the hell cares? We're in the middle of a rehearsal here. I'm about to set up my shots. This goddamn thing shoulda been in the can three days ago!

Buck angrily strides over to the worktable and grabs a copy of the script.

What are you doing?

BUCK: What I shoulda done the first time I saw this goddamn script! (*Starts to tear up script*)

CHARLIE: You can't do that!

BUCK: Yeah? You just watch me! (*Tearing the script and tossing it into a wastepaper basket*) It's a total crock of shit! You're turning her into a goddamn whore! That pipe-smoking son-of-a-bitch is coming out like St. Francis of Assisi, and she's coming out like a goddamn whore!

At the mention of "pipe-smoking son-of-a-bitch," the actor playing the part of Frank strides off in a huff, almost as if he personally had been insulted.

CHARLIE: What difference does it make? Who the hell cares? You're not doing a remake of *War and Peace*! You're doing a lousy reenactment of some whore's murder for cable TV!

BUCK: Shut up, Charlie! Don't tell me what I'm doing!

CHARLIE: No, I'm not going to shut up! You're giving Milly and Nathan everything they want—action, violence, sex! That goddamn script is right on the money, and you know it! So what the hell is coming down here?

BUCK: I want the truth up there, Charlie. The truth!

CHARLIE: I don't believe this. We're filming lousy cable TV one step up from the pornos we used to film for them in the Eighth Avenue bookstores, and you want the truth? You're talking fartsy-craftsy? You better get your head on straight before one of those bastards from upstairs comes down here and cuts your balls off!

BUCK: I want this rescheduled for next week. I'm reworking the script.

CHARLIE: I'm the scriptwriter.

BUCK: Not on this one.

CHARLIE: There's no time open next week.

BUCK: Then make some!

By this point some stagehands have entered to listen to the fight.

(*To stagehands*) What are you waiting for? The A train from 125th Street? I want this goddamn set outta here! Let's move it! We're going in ten minutes with the wino murder!

CHARLIE: Okay. Okay! You want time next week, you got it! You just tell Milly.

Charlie walks over to the actress playing Joy, and throwing up his hands, says something to her. She exits the stage. The stagehands have already begun their work. They will rotate the Joy Bonnard set around on its wheels and place it against the upstage wall, the outside scrim walls of the apartment facing the audience. The "set" for the wino murder, when it is brought in, consists of nothing more than a couple of garbage cans spilling over, a fire hydrant and a single flat painted to look like a graffiti-covered brick wall. These items will be placed directly on the stage floor.

BUCK (*Picking up the worktable phone*): I want an outside line. (*Dials a number*) Hello? Hello, Douglas, this is Buck. How you doing? (*Pause*) Good. Good. Listen, could I talk to Marion for a minute? I've got to make some changes about picking Kenny up. (*Pause, picking up the child's archery set he bought and looking at it until Douglas comes back on the line*) I know she has a headache, Douglas, but she always has a headache when I call, doesn't she? (*Pause*) I'm not being sarcastic, Douglas. I'm being accurate. If I don't pick the kid up with machine regularity, she finds a reason why I can't have him. If I have to switch from a Saturday to a Sunday, it's a big problem. If I'm five minutes late, she's taken the kid someplace for the rest of the day because she thought I wasn't going to show up. Now that's the truth, isn't it?

Charlie, busying himself with some paperwork at the other end of the table, just lowers his head, shaking it.

Why can't we behave like civilized human beings just once, Douglas . . . just once! All I want to do is switch pickup dates! I bought Kenny a little gift and—(*Pause*) Just let me talk to her! Let me explain! (*Pause, then totally losing control of himself*) I don't give a shit if she has a headache! That doesn't stop her from letting me change a date! Douglas? Douglas! (*Jiggling the phone button, but Douglas has hung up. He puts the phone down*)

CHARLIE: Boy, you sure know how to get what you want. Why do you let that son-of-a-bitch stick it to you like that?

BUCK: Mind your own business, Charlie. Maybe I deserve it.

CHARLIE: Nobody deserves it.

Buck picks up the archery set and stares at it again.

What the hell's happening to you, man? Ever since we started on this Joy Bonnard thing. Everything else is in the can in two days. This thing's been going on a week. You're tearing up scripts, you're starting to cost them money. What the hell is coming down?

BUCK: I just want it to be right . . . one lousy thing right.

CHARLIE: It is right! It's just as right as any other reenactment we do. Listen to me, Buck. You came up with a big money winner for them. This murder reenactment idea of yours is the biggest idea to ever hit cable TV, and they appreciate it. All they wanted to do was launder their lousy money through cable, but you showed them how to make a profit. They're grateful. So let it go. Let it go before they dump us back down into the sewer!

BUCK: You should have put in something about her kid, Charlie. The girl at the perfume counter told me she told you Joy Bonnard had a kid.

CHARLIE: Yeah, so what? Who the hell cares what she had beside a pair of tits and an ass?

Shirley, the actress playing the part of Joy Bonnard, enters. She wears a coat and is on her way out.

SHIRLEY: Mr. Halloran? Was I okay?

Buck goes over to her.

BUCK: Yeah. You were fine, Shirley.

SHIRLEY: Mr. Corvanni said you didn't like the way it was going. Maybe if I had a few more lines I could do something better with it.

BUCK: It's not you, Shirley. I just gotta change some things around. You were just fine.

SHIRLEY: You really mean that, Mr. Halloran? I know I'm not much of an actress, but I really feel I understand the part and I want to do the best I can with it.

BUCK: You are, Shirley, and you're just right for it. You're doing a great job.

SHIRLEY: Thank you, Mr. Halloran. It means a lot to me to hear you say that.

CHARLIE: I got a feeling you'll probably get an Emmy nomination, sweetie.

SHIRLEY: I don't expect an Emmy nomination, Mr. Corvanni. I just want to give a good performance, that's all.

CHARLIE: You are, baby, you are. (*Holding up a tape cassette*) I'm gonna get it all down in here. Seven minutes of skin. You're gonna be a big hit in the living room.

SHIRLEY (*Ignoring Charlie's comment*): Mr. Halloran? I'd like to call some agents to see my work. Could you tell me when you think this is going to be shown?

BUCK: I'll let you know next week, Shirley. I really don't know right now.

SHIRLEY: Thank you. I enjoy working for you, Mr. Halloran. (*Starts to exit*)

CHARLIE: If I hear anything about an Emmy nomination, where's the best place to reach you?

SHIRLEY (*Turning and coldly staring at Charlie*): You can't reach me at all, Mr. Corvanni. (*Exits*)

CHARLIE: Ooooh!

Buck has begun sticking tape marks on the stage to indicate to the stagehands where he wants the elements of the wino murder reenactment set placed.

(*Turning to Buck*) You wanna guess where Mr. Milly sent me to find that piece of meat? In the back of a men's boutique in New Jersey! She was wriggling her ass under a pair of five-hundred watt photo lamps while thirteen guys and a cocker spaniel were pretending to take pictures with a Brownie Instamatic. I shoulda left her there.

BUCK: See what's happening with Mr. Goglas and Mr. Berman.

CHARLIE: Bimbos like that really piss me off. You oughta get a load of her bio. She's been stripping since she was fifteen. Smokers in Columbus, lodge halls in Philly, Texas, Oklahoma. That's her chief reference. The high point of her life. Four pornos filmed for Mr. Milly in a bookstore in Philly. You like that? And then she's got the guts to come in here and ask for more lines.

BUCK: See what's happening with Mr. Goglas and Mr. Berman, Charlie. I wanna get going with the derelict murder.

Charlie is fiddling with his camera equipment, still too annoyed with Shirley to sense Buck's mounting anger.

CHARLIE: "If I had a few more lines, I could do something better with it." Jesus, can you believe that? You give a piece of meat like that a chance to wriggle her ass all over the metropolitan area instead of a bookstore porno machine and she's got the gall to ask for more lines.

BUCK (*Blowing up*): I told you to find out what's happening with Goglas and Berman, didn't I? So do it!

CHARLIE (*Replying in kind*): The goddamn suit you want don't fit him! They're still working on it!

BUCK: You check it, Charlie! You check it!

As Charlie walks past Buck.

And the next time you talk to a performer on my stage like that, I'm gonna pick up that fucking camera of yours and bust it over your fucking head, you understand?

CHARLIE: I was just kidding around with her, that's all. You know me.

BUCK: They're on that stage, they're artists, you understand? I don't care where you dig them up from, they're on that stage they're entitled to respect!

CHARLIE: Yeah. Okay. Take it easy.

The brick-wall flat has now been put in place for the wino murder. Charlie stands by the wall and shouts offstage right.

What the hell's happening with the suit?

BUCK (*Still not finished with Charlie*): I'm still the producer around here, not you!

VOICE (*Offstage, answering Charlie in Spanish*): Tu quisiste ojales en los pantalones, así que los estoy poniendo! Tu crees que puedes hacerlo más rápido, pues aquí tienes la máquina . . . y mientras la usas, puedes besarme el culo! [You asked me to put cuffs on the pants, so I'm putting cuffs on the pants! You think you can do it any faster, I'll give you the machine . . . and while you're at it, you can kiss my ass!]

CHARLIE: Then forget about the cuffs on the pants! Just get 'em out here! (*Walks over to the worktable and sits down. Reaching out for a jelly donut, he takes a bite, is disappointed, and puts it down*) Just for once I'd like to get a blueberry one.

For some long moments there is silence between Buck and Charlie, neither looking at the other. When Buck speaks all the anger seems drained away.

BUCK: They got me back in the playground again, Charlie. The same cruddy playground across the street from the apartment I spent five years of my life in with Kenny . . . first rocking him in the carriage, then watching him walk, holding onto my fingers, then one day just going off by himself. And I can see the two of them standing on the terrace, staring down at me through those rotting ficus bushes he planted. And when the reconnaissance is finished with, they move inside for the discussion: "Should we send the kid out, or risk another battle over visitation privileges?" You know how many times I've been to court with them in the last year-and-a-half since the divorce? Four times. Four times! And I always win because we always get the same judge—a sixty-year-old lesbian who knows injustice when she sees it. She issues order after order demanding that I be allowed to see my son. The only problem is it never does any good. My wife has a special dispensation from God which allows her to throw my court orders into the garbage can while I have to obey hers down to the letter of the law or suffer immediate death. "If you don't have him back in four hours, I'll get a court order!" And, by God, she will. She's got an East German refugee with stainless-steel eyeglasses who represents her as a special favor to Douglas's accounting firm. He specializes in court orders. You could call him when he's just starting to boil a soft-boiled egg, and by the time the egg is ready to eat he's got the court order and fifteen documents proving he spent all of World War II as a medic on the Russian front. He keeps dumping me back in the park again with the rest of the divorced leftovers. I sit there watching them waiting for their kids to come out with little gift boxes on their laps, and I'm scared, Charlie. I'm so scared. Scared that they're not going to bring him out to me, scared that if I can't keep up my support payments they'll keep him away from me for good, scared that no matter what I do I'm gonna lose him anyway.

CHARLIE: That's why you gotta keep doing what you're doing, Buck. That's why you gotta give 'em what they want. You start screwing around with them here, they'll get rid of you and they'll get rid of me, and they'll just find somebody else. You'll lose your job, you'll lose Kenny, and it won't change one fucking thing here.

BUCK: He used to circle around the block with his car, waiting for Marion to come out. The last three months of my marriage they didn't care what I knew, what I felt.

CHARLIE: Forget about them, Buck, and listen to me—

BUCK: I hated them so much, Charlie. All I wanted was to walk in on them somewhere . . . in my living room, my bedroom . . . somewhere. That's how I got the idea for my first reenactment, Charlie . . . seeing myself kill them. Did you know that?

CHARLIE: No, Buck, I didn't.

BUCK: Now all I want is just for it to be ordinary again between me and Kenny. But it's never gonna be ordinary again. Ever. The first few months I tried, pretending Saturday or Sunday or whatever the hell day it was they let me see him was just another day of the week . . . but after a while it sinks in. It's gone. The whole damn cord of life that used to hold the two of us together is pulling apart like a piece of wool from an old sweater. And even if I wanted to live with the pretense, I can't, because sure as hell he comes into the park one day and I can see in his eyes he's pretending, too. And he tells me this jerk, this accountant, this Mr. Perfect Mate Lovey-Dovey with three college degrees and a Jaguar, wants him to call him Dad. "Just call me Dad." Well, I told Kenny, "You just call him Douglas. You tell him your dad told you to call him Douglas."

The elevator comes to life with its usual shrill whine and pulsing red light, and Charlie, as usual, is sent into near panic.

CHARLIE: Oh, shit!

Charlie hastens over to his camera, adjusting it for height on the tripod, as the elevator comes to a stop and the door opens. There is a different reality now: Fred Milly is dressed as handsomely as before, only the suit is different; the monstrous club foot has somehow metamorphosed into a simple built-up shoe that compensates for a slight deformation in one of Milly's legs;

the blinding white light that issued from the elevator in the first scene has muted into the ordinary.

How ya doin', Fred?

MILLY (*Coming forward*): Good afternoon, boys. How's it going?

CHARLIE: Right on schedule, Fred. We just finished shooting the death of the girl with the vibrator, and in about ten minutes we're gonna tape the wino murder in the East Village.

MILLY: That was yesterday, Charlie. The girl with the vibrator was yesterday.

CHARLIE: Yeah, that's right. Time sure flies by when you're having fun.

Milly is unamused.

Well, we're right on schedule with the wino. In fact we're thirty minutes ahead of schedule with that.

MILLY: What about the prostitute? The one that got killed by the college professor.

CHARLIE: Buck?

BUCK: We're a little bit behind on that one, Fred. I'll get it in the can by next week.

MILLY: You got a problem?

BUCK: No problem, Fred. We just got a little behind, that's all.

CHARLIE: Cup of coffee, Fred?

Milly just nods his head.

Just black, right?

MILLY: So what's the problem?

BUCK: There isn't any problem, Fred. Just some stuff in the schedule, that's all.

MILLY: The girl I suggested to Charlie working out okay?

CHARLIE: Hey, listen, Fred, she's terrific. You sure know how to pick 'em.

MILLY: I'm talking to Buck, Charlie.

CHARLIE: Yeah. Sure, Fred. Sorry.

BUCK: She's fine, Fred.

MILLY: So what's the problem?

BUCK: There isn't any problem, Fred. I just want to rethink some things.

MILLY: You want me to get rid of her, I'll get rid of her. No problem.

BUCK: She's okay, Fred. Everything's okay.

MILLY: Mr. Nathan likes this one about the whore. He thinks it'll make a good reenactment. He can't wait for it to be in the can.

BUCK: It'll be in the can by the middle of next week.

MILLY: Monday?
BUCK: Tuesday, Fred.
MILLY: Tuesday?

Buck nods.

All right, Tuesday. I'll tell Mr. Nathan he can expect to see it on Tuesday. (*Placing his attache case on the table and opening it up as he speaks*) Mr. Stein wanted me to tell you that he thinks you guys are doing a terrific job. He asked me personally to convey that to you.

CHARLIE: Thanks a lot, Fred. It means a lot to us having Mr. Stein say that.

MILLY: According to the figures on our latest survey, these reenactments have upped our percentage of the cable audience four point seven percent.

CHARLIE: Boy, that's really something, isn't it, Buck?

MILLY: The advertising boys translate this into additional revenues of almost a quarter mil, give or take twenty-five thou.

CHARLIE: That's great, Fred. Old Buck was really on the ball with his reenactments idea.

MILLY: The question now is—where do we go from here? Now that we've grabbed an additional four point seven percent of the market, what's the topper? (*Pausing for a moment as if expecting an answer*) The answer is five point two percent. As Mr. Jacobs put it to me this morning, "We've hooked the magic fish. We've asked him for four point seven percent and he's given it to us. Now we gotta come back and hit him for more." At five point two percent gross revenues punch up to . . . (*Punching in some numbers on his calculator, the calculator noisily printing out the answer*) Three-tenths of a mil.

CHARLIE: Wow!
BUCK: It ain't all numbers.
MILLY: What?
BUCK: I said, everything ain't all numbers, Fred.

MILLY: Sure it is. The height of the Eiffel Tower—nine hundred eighty-four feet. The speed of light—one hundred eighty-six thousand miles a second. The chance of croaking of a heart attack at age sixty-five—one in eight. Everything's numbers.

As Milly continues to speak, one of the actors in the next reenactment, Milton Berman, enters. He is in his sixties and is dressed as a derelict.

You don't pay attention to numbers you end up in Central Park with a pair of baggy pants and a lollipop. Mr. St. George says—

MILTON (*Suddenly calling out, interrupting Milly*): I was promised something to drink!

BUCK: Take it easy, Mr. Berman. (*To Charlie*) Give Mr. Berman a cup of coffee.

MILTON: Not that shit! Something to drink!

CHARLIE: Whatta ya want me to give him, Buck? Your artiste don't want no coffee and donuts.

BUCK: As soon as we're finished with the taping, Mr. Berman, I got a fifth of Johnny Walker for you.

CHARLIE: You hear that, Milton? A fifth of Johnny Walker! You keep your mouth shut and do a decent day's work for us, you're gonna get it. You don't show some respect while Mr. Milly's talking, we're gonna kick your ass out on the street with the rest of the artistes! (*Turning to Milly*) You were saying, Fred, Mr. St. George was saying?

MILLY: Problem: success breeds imitation. CBS, NBC, ABC are getting on their track shoes. They're beginning their own programs. They want to cash in on our breakthrough in the market. Solution? Mr. Stein says—

MILTON: I used to be an engineer!

CHARLIE: That's fantastic, Milton! An engineer! Only I'll tell you something, Milton, you don't look like an engineer to me. You look like a dried-up piece of horseshit! So why don't you keep your mouth shut while Mr. Milly is talking?

MILTON: You got no right talking to me that way! I was an engineer! I was what I said I was!

CHARLIE: So what's the story with you now, Milton? You in-between jobs? You just waiting around to latch onto one of those big engineering jobs? (*To Buck*) That's a lesson for you and me, Buck. You ain't happy with what you got, you're just liable to end up a piece of horseshit, talking about yesterday. (*To Milly*) You were saying, Fred, Mr. Stein was saying?

MILLY: Solution: advance to the next level. So far we've limited our reenactments to local murders. But the public's appetite has been whetted. They're ready to ask us for more, but they don't know yet what more is. Well, gentlemen, Mr. Jacobs says—

MILTON: I had a wife, three kids, and a damn good job as an engineer!

CHARLIE (*Angrily grabbing a newspaper off the worktable and approaching Milton*): Well, then, you know what you need, Milton? A copy of the *New York Times*. It's easy as hell getting a great job. All you gotta do is look in the Help Wanted section.

Charlie throws the newspaper at Milton. Milton throws the newspaper back.

MILTON: I helped build the Verrazano Bridge! I put down the pilings for the Verrazano Bridge!

CHARLIE (*Throwing the newspaper at Milton again*): Then you won't have any trouble getting another job, will ya, Milton?

Milton throws the newspaper back. Charlie, as crazily angered now as Milton, whips open the paper.

I'll even get one for you!

MILTON: I sunk the pilings on the Verrazano Bridge!

CHARLIE: Oh, underwater! You work underwater! I'll get you one for underwater!

BUCK: Charlie!

CHARLIE (*Too lost in his own anger to pay any attention to Buck, pretending to read an ad from the paper*): "Engineer needed for underwater. Long confinement with naked women testing the effects of Johnny Walker Black Label. Interested applicants contact our representative in the main bar of the New York Hilton. Starting salary half a mil a year." You got a dime on ya, Milton? Ya got a dime, I'll make the call!

BUCK: That's enough, Charlie!

CHARLIE: No dime? Gee, what a pisser. Losing out on a swell job like that 'cause you don't have a dime to make a call!

BUCK (*Starting toward Charlie*): I said that's enough, Charlie!

CHARLIE (*Breaking off his attack against Milton, having satisfied his need to publicly humiliate the derelict in front of Milly*): You were saying, Fred, Mr. Jacobs was saying?

MILLY: Expand: the world is big, the world is more. (*Pulling 8 x 10 glossy photos out of his attache case and tossing them one by one on the table*) A school bus blows up in Haifa, children explode into pieces! A Malay strangles a tourist for a pocketful of change in Kuala Lumpur! The wife of a French diplomat is raped and torn apart by communist guerrillas in San Salvador! A South African farmer is gutted by his houseboy in Pretoria, "Freedom" scrawled in blood on the wall!

CHARLIE: Wow! These are great, Fred. Really great.

MILLY: It's our next level, Charlie. Mr. Nathan says—

Mr. Goglas enters to blaring Spanish music coming from the large portable radio he carries on his shoulder. Goglas is in his twenties, thin and supple as a snake.

GOGLAS: Hey, how you like this suit? This is some crazy suit. It don't fit for shit! (*Goes into his dance routine, obscenely thrusting his pelvis*)

CHARLIE: You like that, Buck? That's Mr. Goglas's entrance theme. I found Mr. Goglas dancing in front of a music store on West 50th Street.

GOGLAS (*Pointing to Milton*): Oye! You better give this man a drink. Tu sabes? He don't look so good to me. He's behind in his drinking. (*Putting the radio down*) Hey, papi chulo! (*Walking over to Milton and grabbing his arm*) Come on, let's dance. You look half dead, man.

MILTON (*Pulling his arm free*): Take your hands off me, you son-of-a-bitch!

GOGLAS (*Suddenly snapping open a switchblade*): Come on, man, come on. I'll cut you up!

BUCK (*Hastening over, shutting off the radio*): Put the knife away, Mr. Goglas.

GOGLAS: Sure. Sure. I'm just kidding. You think I'm serious? (*Raising both his arms in the air, a large smile on his face*) I don't cut him up till we get on the camera. (*Closing the knife and putting it away*)

CHARLIE: You were saying, Fred, Mr. Nathan was saying?

MILLY: Devour the world! Go international! Use everything! Everyone!

CHARLIE: God, what a fantastic idea! Look at these photos, Buck. Did you ever see anything as fantastic?

When Buck seems to offer no enthusiasm, Milly walks over to him.

MILLY: Mr. Nathan wants enthusiasm on this, Buck. Real enthusiasm. When he talks about tourists strangled in Kuala Lumpur, he wants to see the juices flow. Mr. St. George says—

Goglas struts over to Milly and thrusts a torn-out page from a porno magazine under his nose. The picture shows a woman lying provocatively with her legs spread apart.

GOGLAS: What do you think of that? She gave it to me. This is my woman. We are getting married. Her father is Don Antonio de Vega Becquer, a rich man. I'm going to make her my queen. What do you think of my woman?

Milly just stares at him. Goglas, seemingly angry, shoves the picture practically into Milly's face.

I ask you something! What do you think of my woman?

For a moment there is silence and it is difficult to say if Goglas is serious or not. Then he laughs, picks up his radio and exits.

CHARLIE: You were saying, Fred, Mr. St. George was saying?
MILLY (*Still not fully recovered from his moment of fright with Goglas*): Mr. St. George thinks—

A stagehand signals Buck.

BUCK: I gotta do the lead-in, Fred. Charlie, I want you on camera.
MILLY: Mr. St. George is talking international, Buck.

The lights snap on over the reenactment set.

BUCK: I have to get on with the taping, Fred.
MILLY: Mr. St. George is talking tourists strangled in Kuala Lumpur, Buck!
BUCK: "A man died in this city . . ." How's audio, Mickey?

Buck gets an okay signal from one of the stagehands who now stands by the monitoring equipment, earphones on his head. Buck holds a white sheet of paper up to the camera.

Gimme a white balance.
MILLY: A South African farmer gutted by his houseboy!
CHARLIE (*Looking at the white paper through the camera*): Got it!
MILLY: The wife of the French ambassador torn apart in San Salvador!
BUCK: Roll tape!
MILLY: Children blown to pieces in Haifa!

Buck stands by the brick-wall flat some feet away from Milton and speaks directly into the camera. Milton, in his role as the derelict, sits on the ground, a bottle of cheap wine in his hand.

BUCK: A man died in this city. A man without a definite name, a definite address. Witnesses to his death remember him only as a man who looked for handouts along the street, a man who cleaned the windshields of passing cars for a few coins to buy a bottle of cheap wine, a man content to sit on the ground and watch through a wine-soaked mind the endless bustle of a great city whirling about him. This man had no part in the life of the city he lived in. There is no record of him in the mission houses, or on the rolls of any city agency. Only now in his death are we, the living, made aware of this invisible man. Only now in his death is this city for the briefest instant of time made aware that it has lost an inhabitant. Only now in his death can we imagine we see him for the first time: the fine network of nerves beginning to form, the skeletal pattern of his bones laid out, the channels of his blood beginning to flow, the bands of fiber and muscle contracting. Only now in the humiliation and death of the invisible man is the measure of our loss made visible.

Buck steps away from the reenactment set as Goglas, playing the part of the murderer, Ramon Luis Carpio de la Barca, enters, dancing to the music of the radio he carries. The derelict watches him.

RAMON (*To the derelict*): Hey! Hey, you! What are you looking at? (*Shutting the radio off and putting it down*) You hear me? I ask you what you're looking at?

The derelict just tries to roll himself into a ball and go to sleep.

Hey? (*Walking over to the derelict*) Hey, you! (*When there's no response he nudges the derelict with his foot*) I'm talking to you!

DERELICT: Leave me alone. I got nothing.

RAMON: What are you looking at me for? You never seen nobody dancing? (*When there is no response he prods the derelict again with his foot*) What are you looking at?

DERELICT: I'm not doing anything to you. Leave me alone.

RAMON: You were looking at me. I don't like people to look at me. You think you can just look at me? (*Kicking the derelict*) Eh? Eh? You better answer me!

The derelict tries to get to his feet, but is pushed down.

You don't look at me because I cannot be looked at! I am the King of the World! You hear what I say to you? Nobody looks at the King of the World unless he tells them to!

DERELICT (*Trying to crawl away*): Get the hell away from me!

RAMON (*Shoving the derelict down with his foot and strutting about*): You see this suit I'm wearing? This is some suit! I don't dress like you dress. This is the only suit like this in the world. I have it because I am King of the World! You understand what I say to you?

DERELICT: You rotten bastard! Get away from me or I'm going to call the police!

RAMON: Whatever I want, I can do! Nobody can stop me! I am the King! (*Squatting down in front of the derelict and pulling out a switchblade*) You see what I got?

DERELICT: Please leave me alone. I don't have anything. I'm nobody. I'm just sitting here.

RAMON (*Snapping the blade open*): You know who gave me this? (*Taking out his magazine photo*) She gave it to me. This is my woman. We are going to be married. Her father is a rich man—Don Antonio de Vega Becquer. I am going to make her my queen. What do you think of my woman? (*Shoving the picture in the derelict's face*) Eh? Eh?

DERELICT: What do you want from me? I haven't done anything. Please.

RAMON (*Standing up and straddling the derelict, holding out his knife*): I could kill you with this and you don't know nothing. You don't feel nothing. When I kill you, I dedicate you to her. I will prove myself worthy of her love by dedicating you to her. (*Raising the picture above his head, looking at it, speaking in Spanish*) Oh, bella reina, yo, Ramón Luis Carpio de la Barca, le dedico a ustéd este toro y mi vida en el nombre de la santa madre de Diós que siempre nos vigila. [Oh, beautiful queen, I, Ramon Luis Carpio de la Barca, dedicate this bull and my life to you in the name of the sacred mother of God who watches over us.]

Ramon squats down behind the derelict and thrusts the picture in front of his face. Charlie, camera off tripod, moves in.

Kiss her feet!

Placing the knifeblade against the derelict's cheek, Ramon forces him into a kneeling position.

I tell you to kiss her feet!

For a moment the derelict just stares at the picture, and then he slowly begins to lean forward.

I am the King of the World and this is my woman whose feet you kiss.

As the derelict kisses the photo, Ramon plunges the knife into his back. The derelict lets out a cry of pain. Ramon lets out a cry of exaltation.

Oh, beautiful queen, I, Ramon Luis Carpio de la Barca, dedicate this bull and my life to you, proving my worth in the name of the sacred mother of God who watches over all things. (*Placing his hand over the derelict's face*) Oh, mother of God, let the blood of this sacrifice pour forth and strengthen our marriage that our life may be fruitful and blessed with many sons. I, Ramon Luis Carpio de la Barca, ask it of you!

Ramon draws the blade of the knife across the derelict's throat. The derelict raises his arms out in front of him as if making a silent plea for help. For a moment the derelict seems frozen into his position, and then he pitches forward, collapsing to the ground as Charlie moves in for a closeup of his face. Ramon bends down, wipes off the blade of his knife on the derelict's coat, closes it and puts it away. Charlie focuses now on Ramon as he picks up his photo and radio. Turning on the radio, giving a final strut and smile to the camera, Ramon exits. Lights up on stage. For some seconds there is no motion, then Milly gets to his feet and snaps shut his attache case.

MILLY: Monday we go international. Monday a Malay strangles a tourist for a pocketful of change in Kuala Lumpur. (*Heads for elevator*)

CHARLIE (*As Milly goes*): I don't think I can find a Malay by Monday, Mr. Milly.

MILLY: Sure you can, Charlie. Check out the Chinese restaurants. New York's full of Chinese restaurants. (*Pressing the elevator button, and then turning around to look at Buck as the doors open*) Oh, by the way, Buck. You know the stuff you did at the beginning . . . the lead-in? (*Stepping into the elevator and turning around to continue looking at Buck*) Mr. Nathan don't like it. Mr. Nathan says talking is a crock of shit.

Milly presses the button to shut the elevator door. Charlie and Buck stare at one another. Sound of the elevator rising as the lights dim and out.

END OF ACT ONE

ACT TWO

The studio, the following week. The movable platform used for the Joy Bonnard living room has now been converted into a dining room to tape the reenactment of "The French Ambassador's Wife Gets Raped in El Salvador." A small table is elegantly laid out with two silver candlesticks, a bowl of fresh cut flowers, some covered silver serving dishes, and a single place setting. Upstage of the table is a large multipaned window, beyond which can be seen the tops of palm fronds.

Bright Caribbean music is heard as the lights come up. A servant (Vincente) enters the room with a covered silver dish. As he enters he gives a slight "out-of-character" nod to Charlie, who is filming the scene. Vincente is in his early twenties, and wears a white serving jacket over his black pants. He places the dish down on the table, stands back to admire the perfectly set table just as a woman (Madam) calls out, presumably from the next room. Music fades.

MADAM (*Offstage*): Jean-Paul? (*Pause*) Jean-Paul?

Vincente stands motionless by the table. In a moment Madam, the French ambassador's wife, enters. She is a handsome woman in an attractive yellow suit, gloves, and a wide-brimmed hat. The suit jacket is cut low enough to expose the top of her generous breasts.

Oh, Enrique, is the ambassador at home?

VINCENTE: Excuse me, madam. I am Vincente. Enrique has left for his vacation.

MADAM (*Really looking at the servant for the first time*): Oh. I don't recall him saying anything about a vacation. How awkward. We are entertaining this evening.

VINCENTE: I'm sure I will be able to perform his duties to your satisfaction, madam. My family has produced a long line of dining-room servants. My great-grandfather worked for the German ambassador, my grandfather worked for the English ambassador, my father was employed by the American ambassador, and, with your permission, it shall be my pleasure to serve you and the French ambassador.

MADAM: But where is the place setting for the ambassador? You have forgotten it.

VINCENTE: No, madam, I have not forgotten it. The ambassador has been called away. He will not be joining you for lunch.

MADAM: Where has he been called away to? He said nothing to me about having to leave.

VINCENTE: His departure was sudden, madam. May I take your hat and gloves?

MADAM (*As she removes her hat and gloves and gives them to Vincente*): I really don't understand what is happening today. First Enrique is not here who is always here, and then my husband is called away and leaves no message for me, and now all morning in the street the sound of gunfire.

VINCENTE: A few malcontents, madam. They come in from the hills, the slums, other provinces. The police will take care of it in a matter of a few hours. It is nothing to concern yourself about.

MADAM: I hope so. This sort of thing is very disturbing. I can't understand what it is your people want. General Rojas is such a perfectly civilized charming gentleman. His government has instituted land reform, social reform, economic reform, elections to take place within two years. What else is it they want?

Having deposited the hat and gloves on a chair, Vincente now returns to Madam in time to help her be seated at the table.

VINCENTE: Some people are just never satisfied, madam. They are never content with what they have. It is in their nature. A condition caused by the constant oppressive heat of the tropics.

MADAM: But the buildings are all air-conditioned.

VINCENTE: Not all of them, madam.

MADAM: You think the answer to this constant unrest is air-conditioning?

VINCENTE: It is impossible to state with any degree of certainty, madam, but it wouldn't surprise me. It is my opinion that this fever in the blood of my people is not caused by social inequality, political fascism, or economic deprivation—but merely by a lack of decent air-conditioning.

Sound of gunfire in the distance.

MADAM: There! Some more of it! This is all intolerable! Absolutely intolerable!

VINCENTE: Shall I serve, madam?

MADAM: What is it the chef has made?

VINCENTE: The chef did not prepare this meal, madam. I did.

MADAM: You? But you are the dining-room waiter!
VINCENTE: In these times we must all play many roles, madam.
MADAM: But where is the chef?
VINCENTE: He has gone also on his vacation, madam.
MADAM: But this is grotesque. I am hosting a dinner party tonight for sixty people.
VINCENTE: The dinner party has been canceled, madam.
MADAM: Canceled? How can it be canceled? Who canceled it?

Vincente lifts the lid to two of the dishes, neither of which appeals to Madam.

VINCENTE: Mushrooms jardinier, madam. Cold bean salad. (*Replacing the lids and lifting a third*) Pâté?

Madam samples the pâté as Vincente puts a little on her plate.

MADAM: What kind of pâté is this?
VINCENTE: Pâté Ambassadorial, madam.
MADAM: It has an odd flavor. I can't quite place it. (*Taking another taste*) It isn't goose liver?
VINCENTE: No, madam, it isn't goose liver.
MADAM: Duck?
VINCENTE: No, madam.
MADAM: It has a slightly gritty texture.
VINCENTE: But not unpleasing?
MADAM: No, it is not unpleasing.
VINCENTE: I would not want to serve madam something that was not up to her usual refined gastronomical standards.
MADAM: Such an odd flavor. I can't quite place it. Is it lamb? Veal? Pig?
VINCENTE: Pig, madam? Does it taste to you like a pig?
MADAM: I don't know. It has a very strange taste. What is it?
VINCENTE: Pâté Ambassadorial, madam.
MADAM: But what is in it? What is it made out of?
VINCENTE: The ambassador, of course.
MADAM (*Abruptly looking at Vincente*): What did you say?
VINCENTE: I said it was made out of the ambassador, madam.
MADAM (*Jumping to her feet*): Oh, my God! My God!
VINCENTE (*Pushing Madam back down in the chair, grabbing her neck in his hands*): But you must finish it, madam. You must finish it all. We are a poor country. We cannot afford to waste any of our food. Your husband and his wonderful French culture, and the

wonderful American culture, and the wonderful English and German cultures, have fed off my country for so long they must be very appetizing. They must be pleasing to the palate! Gastronomical delights!

As Vincente speaks he takes the fork, fills it with pâté and begins pushing it into Madam's mouth. Madam, screaming, tries to spit it out, tries to escape. Charlie, the camera handheld now, moves in for his closeups.

Eat him, madam! Eat him the way he has helped General Rojas devour my people! Eat him the way he has sent in guns and bombs for General Rojas to kill my people! Eat him, madam, the way he has helped stuff our prisons with the innocent! Destroyed lives! Murdered children! (*Shoving the pâté in with his fingers*) Tortured countless victims while you had your dinner parties, fed yourself to the gills, and stopped your ears to the screams of the suffering!

Vincente thrusts Madam's head down so her forehead bangs on the table. Madam gets to her feet, staggering around the room, screaming for help.

Scream, madam bitch! Scream! Add your screams to the screams of my people! No one will hear you!

Vincente slaps Madam so hard she falls against the table, sending everything scattering to the floor. Vincente, spreading her legs, crawls on top of her on the table, ripping open her jacket as he begins trying to rape her.

No one will save you! You who were deaf to the massacre of thousands of my people, pleading, begging your wonderful culture for help, will find no help from the dead! You are now the dead, madam! The raped, maimed, mangled, mutilated dead! And there will be no mercy or forgiveness because you have shown none! Pitiless whore from a pitiless world!

Vincente raises one hand to the sky in a final grandiloquent gesture. Charlie keeps filming for some moments until Buck calls out.

BUCK: Okay, that's a take, Charlie. That's a take.

Charlie stops filming and walks over toward Buck. For a moment neither man notices that Vincente has not stopped his assault on Madam. In fact the assault seems to have grown more real, more violent, the young actor tearing at Madam's jacket, raising the actress' legs, thrusting his groin into her. The actress slaps out hard at him.

ACTRESS (*Screaming*): Get your hands off me, you son-of-a-bitch!

The actress tries to get up, but the young actor holds her down on the table, continuing his assault.

BUCK (*Running over*): I said that's a take! What the hell are you doing?

YOUNG ACTOR: Nothing.

The actress finally manages to push the young actor away and sit up.

ACTRESS: You ever grab me like that again, I'll claw your face into shreds! I'll tear your eyes out, you ignorant bastard!

BUCK: What the hell is going on here?

ACTRESS: He was hurting me! He was purposely trying to hurt me and it had nothing to do with what we were acting! Look what he did to my breast! (*Showing Buck a large scratch on her breast*)

YOUNG ACTOR: You're crazy, lady! I wasn't doing anything to you.

The actress suddenly jumps off the table and starts attacking the young actor with her fingernails.

ACTRESS: You lousy Puerto Rican pimp!

Buck and Charlie have to separate them.

BUCK: All right! Come on! Knock it off! Scene's over! You were terrific! You were both terrific! Take her backstage, Charlie! Get her to cool off!

Charlie has to literally lift the actress off the floor to carry her out. She is still screaming.

ACTRESS: I'll cut your heart out, you lousy pimp! You hear me? You ever lay a hand on me again, I'll cut your heart out!

Charlie and the actress exit. We can still hear her screaming offstage.

Look what he did to my breast! He dug his lousy dirty fingernails into it! (*A final scream back at the young actor*) You lousy dirty Puerto Rican pimp!

BUCK (*To the young actor*): What the hell were you doing to her?

YOUNG ACTOR (*With great hostility*): Nothing! That lousy Park Avenue bitch should be pulled into an alley somewhere! I know people like her all my life! They don't give a shit about anybody! They think they're better than anybody! They come walking down the street with their fur coats and their two-inch-big poodles with diamond collars around their necks and they see somebody like me they cross over to the other side of the street because we're just shit on the street to them! She thinks she can do that to me or my people, I'll pull her into an alley somewhere and show her what she can do! (*Grabbing his genitals and shaking them*)

BUCK: What the hell is the matter with you? She was only playing the part that was written for her!

The young actor continues his tirade, not really listening to Buck. A number of stagehands have come out to watch the action.

YOUNG ACTOR: I'll give her a mouthful of this! That's what she needs, her and all the rest of those Park Avenue whores who think the rest of the world exists to take their hat and gloves!

The young actor throws Madam's hat and gloves in the direction of Buck. The young actor seems genuinely confused and flustered over his own behavior as he stares wildly about him at Buck and the stagehands.

Oh, man!

Picking up the white jacket he had taken off during his assault on Madam, the young actor flees the stage, almost crashing into Charlie.

CHARLIE (*Returning from offstage*): What the hell was that all about?

BUCK (*Truly perplexed*): I don't know.

CHARLIE: She's got a scratch mark from the top of her tit all the way down to her nipple.

BUCK (*To the stagehands*): Let's go! Let's go! I want the Joy Bonnard reenactment set up and ready to rehearse in fifteen minutes. Let's see if we can get out of here before midnight for once!

The stagehands turn the reenactment set around and, rolling it upstage to the back wall, begin converting it into the Joy Bonnard living room. The triptych of panels that had been the ambassador's dining room will be removed, revealing behind them the already-in-place scrim walls of Joy Bonnard's apart-

ment. As the stagehands begin their work, Buck returns to the worktable and Charlie wheels his camera out of the way upstage left past the elevator steps.

CHARLIE: You know what I think? Some of these jerkos can't tell the difference between what they're acting and what's real. The son-of-a-bitch probably thinks we hired the French ambassador's wife for him to rape!

Finishing with his camera, Charlie wanders midstage. For some moments he watches the stagehands busy with their work, and Buck, seated at the worktable, busy with his paperwork.

(*Suddenly blurting out what's on his mind*) Hey, listen, by the way, I gave her the suit.

Buck doesn't answer.

Is that okay?

BUCK: What?

CHARLIE: I gave her the suit. Is that okay?

BUCK: Yeah.

CHARLIE: It's all torn up, but she thinks she can fix it.

BUCK (*Trying to concentrate on the expense figures in front of him*): Fine.

CHARLIE: I figured it was worth it, just to shut her up. (*Pause*) You heard the way she was screaming, and then she started asking about the suit, so I figured what the hell better give her the suit, shut her up.

Pause. No response from Buck.

The way I figure it if Milly or one of those other bastards from upstairs starts asking about what happened to the prop suit, we can always tell 'em the woman was going to sue us and we managed to quiet her down with the suit. Right?

BUCK (*Closing his eyes and rubbing his temples with his fingers*): Right.

CHARLIE: That's the way I figured it too, Buck. (*Pause*) Of course you never know with those sons-of-bitches. You think they'd be grateful we saved them from a lawsuit, but you never know with them. (*Pause*) You don't think that's gonna cause any problems, do you?

BUCK (*Still rubbing his temples as if trying to erase a terrible headache that is getting worse and worse*): What is?

CHARLIE: The suit.

BUCK: Why should the suit cause any problems?

CHARLIE: You ain't listening to me, Buck. I told her she could take the suit.

BUCK (*Finally exploding*): So she took it! She took the lousy fucking suit! Whatta ya want me to do about it, Charlie? You want me to follow her out on the street and tear it off her back?

CHARLIE: No.

BUCK: Because if that's what you want me to do, Charlie, I'll do it! I'll get up right now and do it! (*Standing up and throwing the stack of cost figures in his hand back down on the table*) And fix up your lousy cost figures. There's a four-dollar error in here.

CHARLIE (*Hastening over to the worktable*): On what?

BUCK: I don't know on what! You tell me. If you're going to nickel and dime 'em on the props, you oughta at least learn how to add! (*Walking over to the stagehands and speaking to them*) And make sure there's a white light in that lamp. That apartment gets lit up like a whorehouse again, you're gonna be picking tungsten wire outta your teeth.

The phone on the worktable begins to ring. Charlie just looks at it for a moment as if it might be a rattlesnake shaking its tail, and then picks it up.

CHARLIE: Reenactments. Charlie Corvanni. (*Listens for a moment and then covers the mouthpiece; to Buck*) Your attorney's on the phone. You wanna speak to him?

Buck just throws up his hands.

(*Into the phone*) Hold on a minute. (*Presses the hold button and puts the phone down*)

BUCK: Ask Milly to come down. I want him to see the rewrites I made in the Joy Bonnard reenactment.

CHARLIE: The hell with it. Let's just tape it.

BUCK: I'll tape it after he sees what I've done. Just get him down here.

CHARLIE (*Walking midstage to Buck*): You're making a mistake. As big a mistake as all that revolutionary-crap talk you added to my last reenactment. You already got the word what they think about your crap talk. Whatta ya think Milly's gonna do when he hears that South American banana-eater of yours spouting left-wing bullshit when all he's supposed to do is pull her bloomers off and stick it to her?

BUCK: The man was a revolutionist, Charlie! If all he wanted to do was stick it to her, then he just would have stuck it to her! He wouldn't have spent the morning grinding her husband into a pâté!

Charlie starts to exit stage left.

Why don't you ask yourself what was the meaning of the pâté, Charlie?

Charlie throws up his hands as he exits.

(*Raising his hand to the sky and shouting after Charlie*) The pâté! (*For a moment he just stands there, then walks over to the work-table and picks up the phone*) Hello, Phil. How are you?

As Buck begins his conversation the stagehands wheel the Joy Bonnard set into place downstage and exit. The apartment is different now than when we first saw it: the beaded curtain is down, replaced by a plain cloth one; a number of cheap reproductions of paintings by Degas and Monet hang on the wall; on the mantle there is a collection of photographs; a small imitation Christmas tree complete with tinsel stands on the floor near the phony fireplace. All the changes reflect Buck's concept.

Yeah. Yeah, that's right. I was over Marion's apartment on Sunday. What about it? (*Listens*) No. No. There wasn't any banging on the door, Phil. I just knocked with my knuckle. One knuckle. (*Starts to wander about as he talks*) Oh, that's beautiful. She's got four witnesses willing to testify I was pounding on the door. That's really beautiful, Phil, considering the fact that there's only one other apartment on the floor and I know those people. They wouldn't open their door if the Virgin Mary was being raped by a Nazi panzer division! So what the hell is she trying to pull now? (*Listens*) What kind of court order?

As Buck listens to his lawyer, Shirley enters onto the reenactment set through the scrim door. She wears a pink terrycloth bathrobe and slippers. She holds some pillows in her hand, which she places on the couch. She'd like to talk to Buck, but doesn't want to interrupt his phone conversation.

How in the name of God can she get a court order keeping me outta that apartment house when I'm the one still making the mortgage payments on that fucking co-op the two of them are living in? (*Listens*) No! No! I don't give a damn about her court orders! As far as I'm concerned they oughta take that motto they got chiseled in stone over the courthouse that says "Equal Justice Under the Law," and change it to "Abandon Hope All Ye Who Enter Here!" (*Listens*) If she had brought the kid out to me in the playground the way she was supposed to I never would have gone near that apartment. You know how long I waited in that fucking freezing playground with a bow and arrow on my lap, waiting for her to send Kenny out? Two hours! (*Picking an arrow out of the toy archery set he has just been talking about, and walking around with it and the phone in his hand*) No! There was no confusion. She knew I had to exchange a Saturday for a Sunday because I was working. For God's sake, Phil, doesn't she ever ask herself what would happen to my child-support payments if I lost my job down here because I didn't make myself available when they needed me?

Shirley, without having ever been seen by Buck, exits the reenactment set through the same door she entered. She waits, out of sight, behind the set for Buck to finish his call.

She's got to be flexible! She can't use that as a weapon to keep me from seeing my son! (*Listens*) I want to see him, Phil! Can you understand that? I love him! He's my son and I love him and they won't let me see him! He's growing up and I'm not part of his life anymore! (*Almost broken down in tears, he listens to his attorney. When he finally speaks there is a deadly serious tone in his voice, a frighteningly obvious truth to what he says*) That's right, Phil. You call their attorney and you fix it so I can see my son, because if you don't, I'm gonna go over there and kill the both of them.

Buck hangs the phone up and sits down where his wanderings have brought him—the edge of the reenactment set. As he stares off into space, he keeps jabbing the suction-tip arrow into the reenactment-set floor, over and over again. Shirley watches him for some moments through the scrim door, and then opens the door and pokes her head in.

SHIRLEY: Mr. Halloran?

After a slight pause, Buck looks up.

Can I talk to you for a minute? (*Pause*) It's about the robe.

BUCK: What about it?

SHIRLEY (*Entering onto the set*): I'm not quite sure how I'm supposed to wear it when I come out of the bedroom. When I asked Mr. Corvanni, he told me to ask you because it was your reenactment.

Buck just looks at her.

Should I open the robe a little at the neck so you can see the top of my breasts, or should I open it all the way so you can . . . you know?

BUCK: Just leave it closed. (*Lowering his eyes, staring downward still lost in his own thoughts*)

SHIRLEY (*Starts to exit and then turns back*): I spoke to an agent last Friday. Fred Milly set it up for me. He said he represented a lot of people who are real stars now. At first I thought he was just coming on to me . . . you know what I mean, the way they look at you sometimes . . . but I think he was really interested in my career. We're going to have dinner together next week and talk over how he could get started on a publicity program for me. You know, get me dates with important people, things like that, and then, maybe, have a couple of lines written up in one of the On the Town columns.

BUCK: That sounds terrific, Shirley.

SHIRLEY: I think this agent represents Johnny Carson. At least he had a picture of him on the wall.

For a moment Buck and Shirley just look at each other. Shirley turns to exit, and then finally getting up the courage to say what's on her mind, turns again to Buck.

Mr. Halloran, could I ask you something?

Buck turns around to fully face her, resting his back against the scrim wall. Shirley sits down on the couch.

Do you think I could be an actress? I mean if I went to one of those acting classes and had lessons and really worked at it? Or do you think I'm just fooling myself? You see I've put aside a little money over the years and I wouldn't mind spending it if I thought I had a chance of really becoming a good actress. But if I was just fooling myself . . . it wouldn't be just losing the money . . . you know what I mean? When you stopped the rehearsal last week and I thought it was because of me . . . wow! I just said to myself, "Wow . . . well, shit, Shirley, what did you expect?" And my heart almost stopped.

BUCK: Then you oughta take the chance, Shirley. I think you could be a fine actress.

SHIRLEY (*Sliding down off the couch to a position in front of it*): Because that's what I really want, you know? I've been thinking about it for a long time, ever since I was stripping down in Dallas. . . . I guess Fred Milly told ya about that . . . I mean the stripping part.

BUCK: I don't remember what he told me, Shirley.

SHIRLEY: Yeah . . . well, what it was was that I was always trying to put some words in my act . . . nothing set, or anything like that . . . just what came into my mind. I'd come out and say . . . (*Getting to her knees, snapping her fingers, and in an instant creating her character: a shimmying, breast-jiggling stripper*) "Hi. My name is Francine. What's yours?" (*Stopping her motion and turning to Buck*) That's the name I was using down in Texas. I changed it to Babette in Oklahoma because it sounded more French. And they'd say, "Frank," or "John," or whatever. And then I'd say . . . (*Getting up on her knees again and going through the same routine*) "I need a bodyguard. Would you like to be my bodyguard?" (*Sitting back down again*) You see my full stage name was Francine the Body, so there was a double meaning for the words. I also had a routine I did with a rose. That was when I was supposed to be the Rose of Sharon. You see I had a lot of parts I made up for myself: Babette the French maid . . . the Devil's Angel . . . (*Placing a finger on her hip and making a sound suggestive of heat*) tsss! Very hot! Marie Antoinette . . . (*Drawing her finger across her throat*) Sinderella. *Sin*derella, with an S. . . . When I was Sinderella I showed the whole transformation using little hand puppets like mice to take off my clothes . . . (*Getting to her knees again, making little "eek, eek" sounds as she pretends her fingers are mice pulling at her clothing. Finishing, she sits down again*) But my favorite was the Rose of Sharon. When I was the Rose of Sharon all the decorations on the stage were like petals, and I pinned a rose to the front of my G-string, and then I would lift my skirt and ask if anyone would like to pluck my rose. And someone would always say he would, and try to reach out and grab the rose, but I would never let him. I did it all by myself. (*Lying down on the stage and simulating the action she describes*) I laid down on the stage and I plucked all the petals of my rose and blew them away. (*Sitting up again*) The manager thought it was a good idea because the boys like to say things to you while you're working, and it works out great if you can give them little bits of prop to keep or say things back. Most of the girls just made noises . . . little kissy sounds or things like that . . . but I was the first one there to actually use words, or tell a story.

BUCK: Sounds like you had a really nice act there, Shirley.

SHIRLEY: It was okay. I was doing what I had to do.

There is a silence between them as they look at each other.

Fred Milly tell you why he picked me for this job?

BUCK: I really don't talk much to Fred Milly.

SHIRLEY: I got this job because I was sleeping with him. I told him if he wanted to sleep with me, I wanted to get a job out of it.

BUCK: I hope it was worth the effort.

SHIRLEY: It was.

BUCK (*Standing up*): Listen, Shirley, if you don't mind, why don't we just drop this. I really don't want to hear about Fred Milly's sexual prowess, and I've got some work I've got to finish.

SHIRLEY: He doesn't have any sexual prowess. He stinks. He tries to make love, but all he does is screw. Fred Milly never went to bed with anyone but himself.

BUCK (*Crouching down near her*): Why are you telling me all this, Shirley?

SHIRLEY: You think sleeping with pigs wears it out, Mr. Halloran? You think every time a woman is forced to open her legs to a pig, it wears out what she is? She's something less for it? Because I don't. Not if I was screwed by a hundred different pigs in a hundred different ways would it ever make me feel any less clean or decent inside. They got what they wanted from me, and I got what I wanted from them, and I never gave them anything inside of me that mattered. You're a nice guy, Mr. Halloran. I don't care what the pigs around here think of me, but I do care what you think.

Charlie enters in a semi-run as if the devil might be in pursuit.

CHARLIE (*Shouting at Buck*): You had to give Milly a copy of the new script! We shoulda taped the damn thing as it was last week!

SHIRLEY (*Seeing that her conversation with Buck is about to end, starts to exit*): Maybe we could have dinner together sometime, Mr. Halloran. I'd like that. (*Exits backstage through the scrim door of the set*)

CHARLIE: What the hell did that cuckoo bird want now?

BUCK: Nothing. (*For some long moments he just stares after the departed*

Shirley. Then he turns around and heads over to the worktable) Just something about the robe.

CHARLIE: Yeah? What the hell's the matter with the robe? *(Spraying his mouth with a portable mouthwash, he begins rooting around in the papers on the table)* Goddamn broad thinks she's Marilyn Monroe! *(Sticking his face close to Buck)* Smell my breath. You can't smell any booze on it, can you?

BUCK: No.

Buck watches Charlie pick up the cost figures and start rapidly turning the pages.

What's the matter with you?

CHARLIE: You gave a copy of the script to Milly.

BUCK: Yeah, so what?

CHARLIE: I'll tell you what so what. Nathan saw a copy of it sticking out of Milly's pocket as he passed him in the hall and he pulled it out and read it. And now he's on his way down here with Milly.

BUCK: Nathan never reads anything.

CHARLIE: That's what you think. He had Milly up against the wall and he was grinding the end of his cane into Milly's toes. He was really pissed off. He was grinning from ear to ear.

BUCK: Maybe he was happy about something. People grin when they're happy, too, Charlie.

CHARLIE: Not Mr. Nathan. The last time Mr. Nathan grinned three guys from the fourth floor turned up in New Jersey as part of the foundation for the Meadowlands Raceway. *(Throwing the papers down and picking up another set)* Oh, shit! Oh, shit!

BUCK: Take it easy.

CHARLIE: Don't tell me to take it easy! You couldn't leave well enough alone, could you? We had everything in the world going our way, and you had to fuck it up! You just had to fuck it up like everything else in our lives!

BUCK: What the hell are you looking for?

CHARLIE: The cost figures! Where the hell are they?

Buck picks them up and hands them to Charlie, who immediately flips through them until he locates what he's looking for.

Well, this is wrong. Who the hell said the prop couch cost three seventy-nine? It's only three nineteen. *(Furiously erasing the figure, and shouting as if for the benefit of some unseen presence who might be listening to him)* I catch whoever fucked up these cost figures, he's finished here! He's through! I don't give a shit who he is. I'm not going to take responsibility for somebody else's mistakes!

BUCK: You did the cost figures, Charlie.

CHARLIE: Don't say that! I didn't do these cost figures! I never touched them!

The elevator comes to life with its shrill whine and its pulsing red light above the door. Charlie is thrown into an instant panic as he struggles to right all the wrongs in his cost figures. He keeps glancing at the elevator as he works.

Oh, shit! Oh, shit! Not now! Gimme a second!

Charlie is still talking to himself and trying to fix up the figures when the elevator door snaps open. Milly and Mr. Nathan have arrived. Nathan is a short man in his sixties, spiffy in neither dress nor grooming. The suit he wears is a generation out of fashion, and the sweater beneath it with its row of buttons looks ratty. For a second the two of them stand inside the elevator as if they were posed statues, Milly staring straight ahead, Nathan with his cane in front of him, both hands resting on it. Then Nathan smiles and speaks.

NATHAN: Good evening, my children, good evening. May God be on your side and not grudge you the profits of your labors.

BUCK: Good evening, Mr. Nathan.

CHARLIE: How ya feelin' tonight, Mr. Nathan?

Nathan and Milly come forward, descending the stairs simultaneously, step for step.

NATHAN: Strong, Charlie. Always strong . . . like a pack of Canadian wolves that have brought down a moose, tearing its hamstrings so it cannot run, sinking their teeth into its soft organs, ripping them, eating . . .

MILLY: Mr. Nathan says he feels good tonight, Charlie.

Nathan gives a little wave of his cane.

Mr. Nathan says sit down, boys, sit down, relax.

Buck and Charlie sit down, about as relaxed as a man with a scorpion crawling up his back.

NATHAN (*Sticking his hand in his pocket and taking out some nuts and raisins*): Currants, raisins, seeds?

BUCK: No thanks, Mr. Nathan.

NATHAN: You should eat, Buck. Always eat to keep up your strength for your work.

BUCK: I had a chicken salad sandwich a couple of hours ago, Mr. Nathan.

CHARLIE (*As eager as ever to make points*): I'll have some, Mr. Nathan.

Nathan pours the nuts and raisins into Charlie's outstretched palm. For a moment Charlie just stares down at his palm.

NATHAN: What are you looking at, Charlie?

CHARLIE: Nothing, Mr. Nathan. Just some pieces of lint in here. (*Popping the nuts and raisins into his mouth and chewing*) Boy, these are good. You should try some of it, Buck. Where did you buy this stuff, Mr. Nathan? The health food store around the corner?

NATHAN: No, Charlie. It came with the suit.

MILLY: Mr. Nathan bought the suit secondhand in a bazaar in Damascus in 1967, Charlie, and when he put his hand in the pockets there it was. Isn't that right, Mr. Nathan?

Charlie has stopped chewing, his facial expression turned sour, his teeth seemingly stuck together.

NATHAN: Eat up, Charlie. You waste my time, you waste my life.

Charlie, almost gagging, swallows the food down.

MILLY: Mr. Nathan says his time is limited, boys. He has to fly to Istanbul tonight to discuss international distribution rights for our programming with a Japanese consortium.

NATHAN: I am looking forward to meeting with the Japanese again. (*Walking directly downstage as he speaks*) Kagoshima, Kitakyushu, Nagasaki, Kyoto, Yokosuka, Yokohama, Hamamatsu, Yamaguichi, Wakayama . . .

MILLY: Mr. Nathan has had extensive experience in dealing with the Japanese, Buck. He met them during the war.

NATHAN (*Turning to Buck and pointing his outstretched cane at him*): I incinerated twelve cities! (*Lowering his cane, continuing to speak as he walks behind the worktable*) I blew up dams and drowned the livestock. I razed their shrines and destroyed their gods. I leveled their railroads and their homes, the places where they lived and the places where they prayed. I gave them rack and ruin!

CHARLIE: Boy, I can sure see why you're looking forward to this meeting, Mr. Nathan. Nothing like talking over old times, eh, Buck?

Charlie nervously watches as Nathan begins rooting around in the papers lying on the worktable.

MILLY: It's because Mr. Nathan has this sentimental attachment to the Japanese, Charlie, that Mr. St. George has given him carte blanche to pursue these negotiations to a successful conclusion.

Nathan finds the paper he's looking for, the one Charlie has been erasing. He holds it up to the light, smiles at Charlie, and then sticks it under his arm as he turns his attention to Buck.

NATHAN: You're a good boy, Buck. (*Leaning close to Buck*) Out of the eater came forth meat; out the strong came forth sweetness.

Lifting Buck up by the arm, Nathan walks Buck away from the worktable to a midstage position in front of the reenactment set.

BUCK (*As they walk*): What does that mean, Fred?

MILLY: It means Mr. Nathan likes you, Buck.

BUCK: Thank you very much, Mr. Nathan. I appreciate—

MILLY: I'm not finished with the analysis of Mr. Nathan's remark, Buck.

BUCK: Sorry.

MILLY: Mr. Nathan likes you, Buck, but he's very disturbed that you didn't seek his advice before your marriage went down the tubes. He feels he may have to question the corporate judgment of a man who is too proud to seek help when he needs it.

As Nathan begins to walk back behind the worktable, Milly takes over his spot, standing a few feet away from Buck, staring at him, almost as if riveting Buck to his place.

BUCK: I wish you wouldn't look at it that way, Mr. Nathan. I know I should have come to you, it's just that—

MILLY: Mr. Nathan's not finished, Buck.

CHARLIE: Mr. Nathan sure says a lot in a few words, Buck.

MILLY: Mr. Nathan says a man who feeds his wife with vinegar will suck no honey from her lips.

CHARLIE: Boy, that's really a great thought, isn't it, Buck? Advice like that could really save a marriage.

Charlie, increasingly frightened by Nathan's presence at the worktable, tries to light a cigarette, but everything shakes: his hands, the cigarette, the match.

MILLY: Mr. Nathan hopes you will remember these words of advice as you go forth to seek a new life and a new woman to shack up with.

BUCK: Thank you very much, Mr. Nathan. I certainly—

Nathan crashes his cane down on the table.

MILLY: Mr. Nathan doesn't have time for idle chit-chat, Buck. Mr. Nathan says you are almost ready to move up in the food chain. You do want to move up in the food chain, don't you, Buck?

NATHAN (*Before Buck has a chance to answer*): Oh, Charlie, Charlie. What am I going to do with you? Man that is born of woman has but a short time to live and is full of misery.

CHARLIE: What is he saying, Fred?

MILLY: He's not saying anything, Charlie.

NATHAN: I knew his father when he was running numbers on 125th Street. An honest man from the day he was born to the day he died from ulcers and a liver condition. And now comes the progeny with a couch marked up from three hundred nineteen dollars and ninety-eight cents to three hundred seventy-nine dollars and ninety-eight cents, not including tax! (*Crushing the paper he had taken from Charlie into a little ball and throwing it away, he squeezes Charlie's face in his hands*) Oh, Absalom, Absalom, my son, why hast thou risen against me?

CHARLIE: What's he saying, Fred? For the love of God tell me what he's saying!

MILLY: It's nothing to worry about, Charlie. Absolutely nothing.

NATHAN: Why does he tear my heart out like this? What have I done to deserve this injustice? (*Thrusting Charlie's face away from him in disgust*)

CHARLIE: He's saying something, Fred. He's definitely saying something!

NATHAN (*With mounting ferocity as he raises his hands to the heavens*): Lord, gird up my strength unto the battle! Give me the strength to crush into the earth those that rise up against me! Burn the bones of my enemies into lime! Stone them with stones that betray me! Deliver up their children to the famine! Pour out their blood with the point of a sword!

CHARLIE: It sure sounds like something, Fred. What is it? Some kind of prayer?

MILLY: I don't know what it is, Charlie.

CHARLIE: Buck? Buck?

NATHAN (*Rocking back and forth as he chants*): The heart of the sons of men is full of evil, and madness is in their heart while they live, and after that they go to the dead! (*Hiding his face in his suit jacket*) For to him that is joined to the living there is hope, for the living know that they shall die, but the dead know not anything . . .

CHARLIE: Oh, my God, my God, it's a prayer for the dead, isn't it? He's reciting a prayer for the dead over me! Fred! Fred! Oh, God! Oh, God!

NATHAN: Better a living dog than a dead lion. Better a living cockroach than a dead dog. For the dead rot in the ground and the memory of them is forgotten.

CHARLIE (*Grabbing Nathan's hands, pulling the lapels of the jacket away from his face*): I'll never do it again, Mr. Nathan! I swear to God Almighty I'll never do it again! Just give me another chance! Please, Mr. Nathan, please! I didn't know what I was doing! I didn't! Please! Please!

Nathan pats Charlie on the cheek and then starts to walk away, back to his position near Buck. Charlie tries to follow, to continue his pleading, but Milly steps in front of him, forcing Charlie to sit down again.

MILLY: Mr. Nathan thinks you don't look well, Charlie. He's arranged to have you driven home in his own private limousine. All you have to do is walk out the door and tell the three men waiting for you in the limousine where you live.

Charlie suddenly throws his head back, his hand clutching his chest, his mouth gaping open in what looks like a heart attack. Great gasps of pain come from his throat. Buck, instinctively, starts to move toward Charlie. Nathan blocks his way with his cane.

You live out by the Meadowlands, don't you, Charlie?

At the mention of "Meadowlands," Charlie's agony becomes unbearable. His mouth moves, but only a gasping sound comes out.

NATHAN: What's he saying?

MILLY: What's he saying, Buck?

BUCK: He says he lives on West 55th Street.

MILLY: He says he lives on West 55th Street, Mr. Nathan.

NATHAN: In that case he doesn't need the limousine.

MILLY (*To Charlie*): Mr. Nathan says if you live on West 55th Street, you can just walk home. You won't need the limousine . . . this time.

Charlie, reprieved, struggles to recover from the death sentence. But reprieved or not, Charlie has been totally destroyed. His arms hang limply at his side, his eyes are glazed.

Mr. Nathan is ready to see the rehearsal of the Joy Bonnard murder, Charlie.

Charlie slowly gets up from the table and starts to head backstage. He walks like a dead man.

There's no rush, Charlie. All Mr. Nathan wants you to remember is that you waste his time, you waste his life.

Charlie picks up his pace. Now he stumbles off like a dead man in a hurry. Nathan walks over to the worktable and sits down in the upstage chair, Charlie's chair. Lifting both of his legs onto the table, Nathan heaves out an audible sound of having achieved great comfort. Milly follows Nathan to the table, sits down in the middle chair, and crashes both of his feet down on the table. They both stare at Buck.

BUCK: What you're going to see, Mr. Nathan, is the second scene in the Joy Bonnard murder reenactment. The scene in which she gets killed.

MILLY: Mr. Nathan has varicose veins, Buck. The only way he can get any relief is to lift his legs on top of something. Isn't that right, Mr. Nathan?

NATHAN: This is a great relief.

MILLY: Why don't you put your feet on the table, too, Buck?

Buck walks over to the worktable and, sitting in the remaining chair next to Milly, lifts his legs on the table. Milly has spread his feet so wide there is hardly room for Buck's feet to fit.

Best way to avoid varicose veins, isn't it, Mr. Nathan?

NATHAN: It's a great relief.

BUCK: As I was saying, Mr. Nathan, what you're going to see is the second scene in the Joy Bonnard murder reenactment. The first scene takes place in the bedroom and we're going to be taping that . . .

Buck momentarily loses his train of thought as a strange battle begins between Nathan and Milly. Nathan has just placed his left foot on top of Milly's foot. It rests there unchallenged for a moment.

. . . first thing tomorrow morning. It's going to follow our usual format. Charlie's going to be able to gets lots of . . .

Milly challenges Nathan's foot by lifting his left foot on top of Nathan's foot. There is a big smile on Milly's face as he places his foot down.

. . . skin because both the girl and the man are going to be naked in the bed, and we're going to be able to get lots of good . . .

Nathan drops his remaining foot on top of Milly's. The feet are now stacked up four high.

NATHAN: Muff!
BUCK: I beg your pardon, Mr. Nathan?
NATHAN: Muff!
MILLY: Mr. Nathan wants to know how many good shots of her muff you're gonna get out in this scene.
BUCK: Well, that's the thing, you see, Mr. Nathan. In this scene we're not really going to be concentrating on her muff. We're going to concentrate on her muff in the first scene, but in this scene, the one you're going to see . . .

Milly begins trying to extricate his left foot from the pile. Although Nathan and Milly are smiling at each other, the battle is joined and great pressure is being applied.

. . . I want to pull back the camera, in a sense. I want to show the viewing audience that there was more to this girl than her—
NATHAN: Muff!
MILLY (*By dint of great effort, finally managing to wrench free his left foot*): Excuse me a minute, Mr. Nathan. (*Turning to Buck*) It sounds to me like you're not rowing with both oars on this, Buck. You can't tell Mr. Nathan you ain't shooting—
NATHAN: Muff!
MILLY: Without good muff shots we lose seventeen percent of the viewing audience.
BUCK: I understand that, Fred.
MILLY: Ass eleven percent, tits fourteen percent, muff seventeen per-

cent. It's all in the computer, boy! (*Dropping his left foot on top of Buck's right*)

BUCK: If you'll listen to me for a minute, Fred, I'll try and—

MILLY: Because it sure sounds to me like your elevator ain't got no top floor, Buck. Your refrigerator door's open, but the light ain't comin' on!

Buck begins struggling to extricate his foot as he argues with Milly, but Milly is tenacious.

BUCK: All I'm trying to say is that we gotta start putting these pieces of people together so that some kind of whole human being comes out. You can't keep breaking people down into tits and muffs and say that's all there is to them!

Buck continues to violently try to pull his foot out from under Milly's foot, but Milly holds on.

MILLY: The hell we can't, boy! The twenty-one percent share of the cable market we've grabbed sure as hell says we can!

BUCK: I'm not talking about market shares, Fred! (*Giving up trying to extricate his right foot, Buck drops his left foot on top of Milly's foot*) I'm talking about meaning! I'm talking about the meaning of human life!

Milly looks from one of his legs to the other, suddenly realizing he is spreadeagled on the table—his right leg held down by Nathan, his left caught in a scissors grip by Buck's feet. He tries to pull his feet free, but Nathan and Buck hold on.

How long can you keep filming people cut up into butchered parts, Fred? How long can you pretend human life is nothing better than dead organ meat?

Nathan slips his cane under Buck's and Milly's legs and begins pulling them closer to him.

If we see people die and then we take away everything that gave their life meaning, what is there going to be left for any of us, Fred? What is there going to be left when the world has pulled itself down into a sewer, Fred?

As all the feet are brought together, a tremendous melee of thrashing legs breaks out in a battle for dominance. The battle continues for some seconds, reaches its frantic pitch, and then suddenly stops: Buck's feet on the bottom, Milly's feet in the mid-

dle, Nathan's feet on top. Nathan, in triumph, pokes his cane into the air, screaming out as if in answer to Buck's question.

NATHAN: Muff! Muff! Muff!

Lights dim on the worktable and come up full on the reenactment set.

JOY (*Offstage*): You make me feel like dirt! You make me feel like a whore!

Entering the room through the archway, Joy is in a highly agitated state. She moves about the room for some moments, making spastic little motions with her hands, shaking her head, before she finally comes to a stop by the phony fireplace. She has obviously been crying. She wipes her eyes. Frank enters barefooted and wearing only his briefs.

FRANK: What the hell is happening here? It's one in the morning. Let's get back into bed. I'm not finished yet. (*Waits a moment for an answer, and when there isn't any, comes forward*) I don't know what the hell you're trying to pull, but I don't have time for this. I gotta get outta here in a couple of hours. I got a paper to deliver at the MLA convention in the morning. I told you that. So come on, let's go. I'm ready to go again. (*Grabbing at her arm when she doesn't answer*) Did you hear what I said?

JOY (*Pulling her arm free*): Keep your hands off me!

FRANK: I told you I'm ready to go again, so let's do it!

JOY: No!

FRANK: Don't tell me no! Two lousy fucks and that's supposed to be it? Well, let me tell you something. Two lousy fucks isn't worth the cab fare it cost me taking you home! (*Pulling her*) Now come on!

JOY (*Wrenching her arm free again and moving away*): Get out of here! Why don't you just get your clothes on and get out of here! I'm not your whore! I'm not any man's whore! So just leave me alone!

FRANK: Sure, I'll leave you alone . . . when I'm finished.

JOY: You're finished now! I'm not getting back into that bed with you!

FRANK (*Grabbing both her arms, his anger suddenly boiling up to terrifying proportions*): Don't you tell me what you're gonna do! Don't you ever tell me what you're gonna do! (*Thrusting her violently down on the couch*)

JOY: I thought we could be good for each other! I thought because you had an education you would be capable of some sensitivity! I could get the smallest touch of understanding from you!

FRANK: Who the hell do you usually pick up in that bar? Leonard Bernstein? The Sultan of Morocco? Rimski Korsakov? Why don't you get off your high horse and take a good look at yourself? You're nothing! Nobody! A hole walking around on two legs, too stupid to even realize that the only reason any man ever comes up here is just to stick it to you!

JOY: That's not true! The only men that ever came here were men that I wanted here . . .

FRANK (*Beginning a litany that continues throughout her reply*): Stick it to you! Stick it to you! Stick it to you!

JOY: Men I invited up here because I thought a relationship might develop, something worthwhile, something. . . . Stop it!

FRANK: I'll tell you the kind of men you brought here. The scum of the earth, stinking of liquor and sweat. Tired old men with bloated bellies and suspenders—

JOY: Why are you doing this?

FRANK: Teenage jocks from the garage with car grease dripping from their fingers, and their tongues lolling outta their mouths like the bovine numbskulls they are.

JOY: Why are you turning what we could have felt for each other into a sewer?

FRANK: And you took them home with you, and you let them stick their fingers into every crevice of your body. And you took them to bed with you and you lay there next to them and under them, laughing at their moronic jokes.

JOY: They were decent men!

FRANK (*Kneeling down on the couch beside her, pressing his face close*): But that's what every whore tells herself, isn't it? Lying there in the dark while those sweaty stinking bodies pound down on her. "I am the Snow Queen and Prince Charming has come to slide his bloated tongue into my mouth!"

JOY (*Standing up and moving a few feet off to get away from him*): And what did you do with your tongue? And what hole in my body didn't you shove your fingers into? What am I guilty of, Frank? Thinking you would turn out to be different than the rest of them? Believing there was a chance I could meet someone capable of giving love for love? Was that my crime, Frank? Not believing that love is shit and people are scum?

Frank covers his face with his hands, rubbing his eyes, his temples, as if trying to soothe a terrible headache.

All the way home in the cab I thought how good tomorrow was going to be with you: waking up, going to the hotel, listening to you deliver your paper. I was going to be there for you, to listen to you. I wanted that because you made me feel in the bar that you were someone I could open my heart to. That everything was possible. What was that all about, Frank? Just to turn it into a screw job in a fourth-floor walkup, without any gentleness, without any meaning—like an animal? Well, how dare you do that to me? How dare you do that to any human being? I have love inside of me, and poetry inside of me, and—

FRANK: The hole that walks on two legs has poetry inside of her? (*Standing up and walking over to her*) What kind of poetry? Hallmark cards? "Trees"?

JOY: If you wanted a whore, Frank, why didn't you just pick up a whore? Why did you come looking for someone like me?

FRANK (*Ignoring her remark, or pretending to*):

"I think that I shall never see
A poem lovely as a tree,
A tree that may in summer wear
A nest of robins in her hair . . ."

Frank runs his fingers through his hair to show what it would be like having robins walking around in your hair. Joy sits down on the couch, turning away from him.

Now that we've exhausted everything you know about poetry, maybe you'd like to talk about philosophy? Maybe you'd like to enlighten me with your perceptions on Schopenhauer, Nietzsche, the will to live and the will to be Superman. I could use it in my lecture tomorrow. No? How about a thousand words on Kafka and Camus, Jean-Paul Sartre and the failure of existentialism to solve anything? Yes? No? What do you want to talk about? Polly wanna cracker? Talk. Talk. Squawk. Squawk. You tell me what the salesgirl behind the department-store perfume counter thinks anybody would be interested in hearing her talk about? (*Silence*) That's right! Zippo! Nada! Nothing! (*Opening the liquor cabinet and pouring himself a drink*) God, this whole stinking society makes me sick! Always whining. Always bellyaching.

Frank swallows down the drink. For some moments there is nothing but silence between them as Frank stands there, facing away from Joy.

JOY: You're as lonely as I am, aren't you, Frank?

For some moments more Frank stands there rigidly staring forward. But the question has been heard and has had a visible effect upon him. He suddenly turns toward Joy.

FRANK: Come on. Let's get back into bed. It's colder than hell out here. (*Squatting down in front of her*) Didn't I show you as nice a time as you showed me? (*Opening the bottom of her robe*) Wasn't that a nice couple of sweet screws we had? (*Stroking her legs, kissing them*) Such beautiful legs . . . such sweet beautiful legs . . . I just wanna bury myself in them.

As Joy watches Frank burying his face between her legs, a slight smile comes to her face; but it is not a pleasant smile, and her eyes are filled with ice and hate.

JOY: Do I excite you, Frank? Does it excite you being here with someone like me?

FRANK (*Too lost in his passion to really pay attention to what Joy's saying, or sense the change that has occurred in her*): Yes.

JOY: So much nicer than having to stay in that stuffy hotel room, or that stuffy little university town where you teach, isn't it, Frank?

FRANK: Yes.

JOY: Having to pretend all sorts of things to all sorts of people all the time, when you can come down here and get off on the crumpled sheets of an unmade bed.

Frank tries to climb up on the couch beside her, but Joy places her foot against his chest and pushes him down to the floor.

But you gotta stay down on the floor, Frank. If you wanna get a good look at everything I am, you gotta stay down on the floor.

Joy straddles Frank, sitting on his chest.

FRANK: I like it when you tease me. When you pretend you don't want it and you make me work for it.

JOY: I can do anything you want, Frank. I know lots of tricks.

FRANK: (*Squeezing her breasts*): Oh, God, this feels so good. Your boobs feel so good in my hand.

JOY (*Grabbing his wrists and forcing his hands away*): I want it too, Frank. I want it as much as you do, but we have to settle the money thing. We have to get the money thing out of the way so we don't have to think about it.

FRANK: I just want to squeeze them . . . kiss them . . . suck them in my mouth . . . no thought . . . no thought anymore . . . oh God, just kiss, just—

Lowering her head as if to kiss him, Joy spits in his face. Before Frank has a chance to react, she moves away, sitting down on the couch.

You whore! You lousy whore! (*Getting to his feet, and wiping the spit off his face*) You're like all the rest of them! Every face I have to face in the lecture hall!

Frank goes over to Joy and rubs the spit from his hand into her face. Joy jumps to her feet, trying now to get out of the room, get away from Frank as he stalks after her.

A universe of dull, boring, whining, stupid mediocrities! And I watch them filing in every day . . . (*He pushes the couch so Joy is blocked against the fireplace wall*) And I'm like a god to them . . .

Joy tries to climb over the couch and run past Frank, but he grabs her, pulling her down to the floor, choking her.

And I let them feed from the trough of my intelligence: the loudmouth and the bully, the coward and the cunning, the pathetic, the false, the debased, the insignificant!

Joy, desperately trying to save herself, reaches out for one of the knitting needles stuck through the half-finished sweater lying near the arm of the couch. Frank grabs her wrist before she has a chance to strike out at him, and turning the needle around in her hand, begins driving it down into her chest.

Dismal gray eaters of another man's intelligence! And before them I spread out the feast of my skull, my consciousness, my being . . . and year after year I watch them dine on all the dainties . . . munching me, tearing me, sucking out the marrow of my existence! And when the year is over they leave, and a new horde of useless, brainless—

As the needle drives into Joy's heart, she screams—and for a long moment her scream rends the air.

They're eating me alive! They want me to have answers and I don't have any answers! They want me to be God and all there is to me is a sack of testicles between my legs!

Frank, almost in tears, lies down against the still body of Joy Bonnard. For some seconds there is only silence. Nothing moves. Then the stage lights abruptly come up. Milly, Nathan and Buck, their feet on the floor now, are still seated at the worktable. For some moments more the silence continues as Nathan stares at the reenactment set and the drama that has been played out for him. Buck looks over at Nathan, trying to read some reaction.

BUCK: As I said, Mr. Nathan, this is only part of it. I'm going to have the introduction, and then there's the scene between the two of them in bed. I just wanted to show you this particular scene because I think it helps us understand something of what Joy Bonnard was really like as well as some of the motivations of the—

Nathan scrapes his chair back as he gets to his feet, the sound cutting Buck off in mid-sentence. Nathan looks at Buck for a moment and then walks over to the reenactment set, Buck trailing, pleading his case.

She was a decent human being, Mr. Nathan. She went into that bar, she drank, she took men home with her, but it wasn't because she wanted money from them. It was just something to push away the loneliness that was in her life.

Under Nathan's withering glance, the actor playing the part of Frank quits the stage. Buck seems even more desperate now.

She was suffocating, Mr. Nathan, and she couldn't find anyone to listen to her! She listened to all those men, but which one of them ever listened to her? Which one of them—

Nathan abruptly turns and heads for the elevator. Buck stares at Shirley, left alone on the stage, and then she lowers her head and exits.

You can't walk away from it, Mr. Nathan! You can't pretend the agony of the world doesn't matter!

Nathan enters the elevator, followed by Milly. They turn around to look at Buck.

You do that you're gonna wake up in the middle of the night, crying out for the sound of a human voice, and all that's gonna come back to you are the screams of baboons rubbing their asses on the ground!

MILLY (*Continuing to look at Buck for a moment longer*): Mr. Nathan says . . . throw the garbage out and shoot what you had last week.

Milly presses the elevator button. The door shuts and the elevator begins its shrill ascent. Buck takes the toy arrow he's been carrying around in his hand and throws it at the elevator. It harmlessly bounces off the shut door. Charlie, seeing the coast is clear, enters. He thrusts out his hands, still trembling.

CHARLIE: Boy, look at that! They're shaking like a leaf.

Buck sweeps his arm across the worktable, sending a pile of papers flying.

When he started reciting that prayer for the dead over me, I thought for sure I'd bought it. I thought for sure I was going to be part of the Meadowlands. He wasn't kidding, was he, Buck?

BUCK: No.

CHARLIE: Wow! I'll tell you something—this was worse than what happened to me last week. I woke up in the middle of the night, grabbing my guts. I couldn't believe it. I thought my insides were coming out. I didn't know what the hell it was. I ended up crawling on the bed on my knees, bent over like some goddamn Moslem bowing to a prayer wheel. I was going around like that for two hours: in the bed, in the tub, walking around. The pain was terrible. First it was in the kidneys, then it was in the side, then it was about three inches over the groin. I thought something blew up in there. I was scared, I don't mind telling ya. I thought I really had it. I thought I was going to the hospital, the whole works! And then you know what it turned out to be? Gas! Would you believe it? Gas! I sat down on the toilet and let out a fart that almost blew the door off the wall. I was never so happy in my life. That's the way I feel now, Buck. This is the happiest moment of my life!

BUCK: Go on home, Charlie.

CHARLIE: Yeah. Sure. What the hell time is it anyway? (*Looking at his watch*) Christ, it's after midnight, already.

Charlie hunts around the elevator steps for his rubbers as Buck walks over to the reenactment set.

What the hell did I do with my rubbers? The radio said it was going to snow like a son-of-a-bitch tonight. (*Finding his rubbers under the steps, he sits down and puts them on*) So whadda ya gonna do now?

Buck bends down and picks up the knitting needle. He holds it in his hand, staring at it.

You want me to clear some time to shoot the Joy Bonnard thing on Friday?

BUCK: Yeah. Sure. Friday's fine, Charlie. (*Wanders for a few moments about the set*)

CHARLIE (*Putting on his leather jacket and winding a muffler around his neck*): We can shove it in right after the tourist gets strangled for a pocketful of change in Kuala Lumpur. Or is it the school bus that gets blown up in Haifa on Friday? I can't keep the fucking things straight anymore.

BUCK (*Coming to rest on the arm of the couch*): It's the school bus on Friday, Charlie.

CHARLIE: Yeah, that's right. I keep thinking about this piece of meat I've got coming in to play the part of the tourist. She's gotta go two hundred pounds, but when she sits there in the tub with her balloons floating on top of the water, the shot I'm gonna get looking down is gonna be unbelievable. When she gets strangled and goes under, the fadeout's two nipples comin' up to the surface. You got any idea what half those clown directors they got in Hollywood would give to come up with a shot like that? Their left nut! But they didn't do it. Charlie Corvanni did it! Charlie Corvanni working for Shit Enterprises did it! (*Clapping his hands as if trying to work up some exuberance in Buck*) Okay! So Friday it is! (*Walking over to Buck and touching him*) Listen to me, old Buckeroo. It just don't matter. By the time we do a reenactment of it they're all dead anyway. You're dead you don't have to give a shit about anything. (*Turns and starts to exit*)

BUCK: It's going to be pretty out there tonight, Charlie, with all that new snow coming down.

CHARLIE: Sure. And by tomorrow morning when they get done sanding it and a million bums get done pissing into it, it's gonna end up like it always ends up—a pile of sopping shit!

BUCK: That's right, Charlie. That's just what happens to it.

Charlie exits.

The wonder of it is is that it ever bothers coming down at all.

Lights fade and out.

END OF PLAY

SWEET TABLE AT THE RICHELIEU

For Robert Brustein.

Sweet Table at the Richelieu was first presented by the American Repertory Theatre in Cambridge, Massachusetts, February 6, 1987. Andrei Serban directed. The sets and costumes were designed by John Conklin, the lighting by Howell Binkley and the sound by Stephen Santomenna. The cast was as follows:

Jeanine Cendrars .... Lucinda Childs
Frau von Kessel .... Elizabeth Franz
Driver .... Ken Howard
Cathy/Lieder Singer .... Lynn Torgove
Henri Dusseau .... Nestor Serrano
Estelle Dusseau .... Sandra Shipley
Mrs. Karras .... Isabell Monk
Anthony .... Harry S. Murphy
Lester .... James Andreassi
Dr. Atmos .... Jeremy Geidt
Mimosa Klein .... Harriet Harris
Franco Boupacha .... Thomas Derrah
Gabriella Bottivicci .... Pamela Gien
Cesare Bottivicci .... Ken Howard

Ronald Ribman created *Sweet Table at the Richelieu* and was an artist-in-residence at the American Repertory Theatre through the generosity of the National Endowment for the Arts/Fellowships for Playwrights program.

CHARACTERS

JEANINE CENDRARS
FRAU VON KESSEL
DRIVER
CATHY
HENRI DUSSEAU
ESTELLE DUSSEAU
MRS. KARRAS
ANTHONY
LESTER
DR. ATMOS
MIMOSA KLEIN
FRANCO BOUPACHA
GABRIELLA BOTTIVICCI
CESARE BOTTIVICCI

PLACE

Scene 1: The woods before the Richelieu.
Scene 2: The grand entrance hall of the Richelieu.
Scene 3: The great room of the Richelieu.

Scene 1

The woods before the Richelieu. In the semidarkness a young woman, Jeanine Cendrars, anxiously paces back and forth. The coat and hat she wears seem poor protection against the freezing wind that blows. Suddenly, in the distance, the sound of a fast-approaching sleigh: horse hooves beating into the snow, whip cracking, sleigh bells, a woman crying out.

FRAU VON KESSEL: Watch where you're driving the sleigh, you oaf! The road is strewn with rocks, the branches are whipping into my face! (*The sleigh comes to a stop. The woman continues screaming as the lights gradually come up*) Elegance has gone out of the world! Order, discipline! Il n'est plus ici, le concierge! Replaced by jackasses, buffoons, nonentities with the charm and civility of sandpaper! The world can drown in the sun for all that's left of value!

Lights up full. The driver of the sleigh is a huge wild-looking bearded man dressed in fur. In his hand he holds a long vicious whip. His passenger, Frau Von Kessel, is an elderly sour-faced woman dressed in a heavy fur coat and wrapped about in a thick blanket. For a moment, Frau Von Kessel either doesn't see Jeanine Cendrars, or else has purposely chosen to ignore her as she continues to vent her spleen on the driver.

Why are you stopping here, you idiot? (*Slowly turning her head toward Jeanine, staring at her for some seconds, and then suddenly stabbing her finger out at her*) You! Don't just stand there! If you're for the Richelieu get in! Get in the sleigh before this snowstorm tears the skin from my face!

Jeanine approaches the sleigh with trepidation and uncertainty, staring at the woman and the fierce driver.

Well? Get in! Get in! What is the matter with you?

JEANINE: I took a wrong turn in the woods.

FRAU VON KESSEL: I don't have the patience to listen to your petty twaddle! Are you for the Richelieu, or not? (*To the driver when Jeanine doesn't respond fast enough*) Allez! Allez! Leave her in the snow!

As the driver raises his whip to lash out at the horses, Jeanine scurries aboard the sleigh. Frau Von Kessel waves her cane.

Allez! Allez!

The whip descends in a crack, the bright daylight becomes blue-white, and the sleigh races on, Frau Von Kessel continuing her diatribe.

The summer has been abysmal! The fall no better! The ferry-crossing over the Bosporus ruined by carbon monoxide!

JEANINE: I feel so cold.

FRAU VON KESSEL: Greece no better! Skiros, Khios, Naxos reduced to pissholes in the Aegean, pawed over by Americans in Frye boots!

JEANINE: Could we share the blanket? I'm so cold.

FRAU VON KESSEL: It's not large enough.

JEANINE: But it's wrapped around you twice.

FRAU VON KESSEL: That's exactly what I need for my comfort.

JEANINE: But you have a fur coat.

FRAU VON KESSEL: It's not enough. Everything is not enough!

JEANINE (*Slightly tugging at the blanket*): If you would just give me a little of it. It's a hotel blanket.

FRAU VON KESSEL: Leave it alone, you American wimp!

JEANINE: Can't you see it's not fair that you should have a fur coat and a blanket, while I have nothing?

FRAU VON KESSEL: It is perfectly fair! My husband is the Herr Baron Ernst Von Kessel! We are related to the Krupps! This blanket is mine!

JEANINE: This blanket belongs to the hotel, Mrs. Von Kessel. You see, it has the hotel's name on it. All I'm asking for is just enough to cover my legs.

FRAU VON KESSEL (*Raising her cane*): I'll warm your legs with this if you don't let go this instant! It should be enough for someone like you to just share a carriage with me!

JEANINE (*Continuing to pull at the blanket*): I'm only asking for what's fair.

FRAU VON KESSEL: You'll pay for this!

JEANINE: Please, Mrs. Von Kessel. There's plenty for the both of us. Surely we can share it.

FRAU VON KESSEL: My husband will destroy your husband! My children your children!

JEANINE: Why are you being so mean?

FRAU VON KESSEL (*As the battle for the blanket continues to rage*): I'll have your tubes tied for this! I'll have your milk glands dried! I'll see to it you never give suck again! The Von Kessels forget no injury! Forgive no insult!

Jeanine wins the battle by suddenly, inadvertently, pulling the entire blanket off Frau Von Kessel.

JEANINE (*Immediately conciliatory*): We can share the blanket. I'll just spread it out over the both of us.

As she starts to do so, the sleigh comes to an abrupt stop in front of the Richelieu. Bright daylight returns. Frau Von Kessel angrily thrusts the blanket aside.

FRAU VON KESSEL: It's too late trying to worm your way back into my favor! We have arrived at the Richelieu! You have not heard the last of this! (*To the driver, who has descended from the sleigh and is in the process of removing her luggage*) Well, what are you waiting for? Do you expect me to walk through this unshoveled muck? Pick me up! Carry me into the hotel! Schnell! Schnell!

The driver, with a large suitcase belonging to Frau Von Kessel in one hand, lifts her out of the sleigh with his other arm about her waist, jostling her as he adjusts her for balance. Tucked under the driver's arm, Frau Von Kessel continues her tirade at Jeanine.

I never want to see you again! I never want to hear the sound of your voice again!

JEANINE: But we are staying in the same hotel, Mrs. Von Kessel.

FRAU VON KESSEL (*Raising her hand to her eyes as if to shade them from a glaring sun, looking around and through Jeanine, pretending she doesn't see her*): Did someone speak? Was there someone who spoke? I see no one. (*Sharply to the driver*) Allez! Allez!

The driver, with Frau Von Kessel and her luggage under his arms, starts to exit toward the hotel entrance.

Watch what you're doing with my luggage! I don't want it getting wet in the muck!

Under the strain of his load, the driver's luggage arm dips perilously close to the ground. The whole operation seems jerry-rigged, teetering, in danger of collapse.

You're getting my luggage wet, you simpleton! Lift your arm! Your arm!

The driver lifts the wrong arm, the arm holding Frau Von Kessel.

Not that arm, you moron! The arm with the luggage in it!

Frau Von Kessel, driver, and luggage vanish offstage, reeling, lurching, pitching, her final remark wafting back.

Où est le concierge?

Jeanine remains in the sleigh for some moments after they are gone, and then she steps down from the sleigh and quickly exits after them into the hotel. Blackout.

Scene 2

The grand entrance hall of the Richelieu. Two fluted columns with plush red velvet cushions about them stand at stage left and stage center. At stage right is the reception desk. Seated at one column is Estelle Dusseau, a well-dressed, impeccably coiffured woman in her late thirties. She appears downcast, her hands folded in front of her, her eyes gazing at the floor. Occasionally she steals a glance over toward the man seated at the other column, her husband, Henri. Henri, in his elegant afternoon suit, his cufflinks, his pencil-thin mustache, is in a very angry mood at the moment. He reads his newspaper, rattling the pages as he turns them. Whenever his eyes meet his wife's, he grows angrier and angrier. Estelle Dusseau has been crying; but no matter how soft her sobs, how delicately she raises her handkerchief to her tears, he remains adamant in his mood. When he has been inflamed beyond forbearance, he strides over to her, taps her on the arm with the folded newspaper as if trying to force her to leave. When she remains in her place, he fumes for a few moments, and then returns to his seat, his back further toward her, his newspaper rattling louder than ever. Frau Von Kessel enters, tucked under the arm of the driver. As soon as she and her luggage have been deposited in front of the reception desk, Frau Von Kessel begins ringing the little desk bell for service. Jeanine enters, staring about her at the elegance that stretches everywhere. She comes to a halt at a respectful distance behind Frau Von Kessel just as the desk clerk, a beautiful young girl named Cathy, enters.

FRAU VON KESSEL (*To Cathy*): This hotel has deteriorated since my first treatment here in 1936! Be warned! The world is filled with modern mineral baths! One is no longer obliged to come to the Richelieu for rejuvenation! (*Glancing with disdain at Jeanine behind her before turning back to the desk clerk*) If you do not exercise caution with the clientele you admit, you will be without the clientele you wish to admit! I am the Frau Baron Ernst Von Kessel. Are my rooms ready?

CATHY: You are out of order.

FRAU VON KESSEL: What?

CATHY: You will have to wait your turn. (*Gesturing with an open palm toward Jeanine*) This lady is first.

FRAU VON KESSEL (*Turning around*): I see no one.

Turning back to the desk clerk as Jeanine takes a hesitant step or two forward.

How can that . . . person . . . be first when it is I who am standing here in front of you?

CATHY: Please step aside until this lady has had a chance to register.

FRAU VON KESSEL: Are you insane? Did you not hear me when I told you I am the Frau Baron Ernst Von Kessel?

Ignoring Frau Von Kessel, the desk clerk smiles kindly at Jeanine, gesturing again for her to approach the desk.

CATHY: Welcome to the Richelieu, Mrs. Cendrars. It's so nice to have you with us again. (*Jeanine just stands still*) You don't recognize me, do you? I'm Cathy, Mrs. Cendrars. We met when you were here with your husband on your honeymoon. I was twelve years old then. We went skiing one afternoon, just us, in the mountains.

JEANINE (*Suddenly remembering, a happy smile breaking out on her face as she comes forward*): Yes! Yes! I do remember you! But you've grown so much! You're a beautiful young woman now!

CATHY: It's been seven years. (*Holding out her hand to show a diamond engagement ring*) I've gotten engaged.

JEANINE: Oh, how beautiful! You must be so very happy.

CATHY: Yes, I am. As happy, I hope, as you were when you first came here. I feel as if my whole life is just beginning.

FRAU VON KESSEL: How much longer am I going to have to listen to this tedious drivel? I wish to be taken to my rooms, immediately!

CATHY: I'm afraid you don't have a reservation.

FRAU VON KESSEL: Of course I have a reservation.

CATHY: There is no reservation for you, Frau Von Kessel.

FRAU VON KESSEL: This is monstrous! I have been coming here for fifty years for my rejuvenation treatments, and there is always a reservation understood for me.

CATHY: There are no longer any understood reservations, Frau Von Kessel. I'm sorry. (*To the driver*) Please carry Madame Cendrars' luggage up to the bridal suite.

FRAU VON KESSEL: But that is my suite! I have always stayed in the bridal suite!

JEANINE: I have no luggage.

CATHY (*Pointing to several pieces of fine luggage by the desk*): Oh, yes. It's all been forwarded on ahead. Everything has been taken care of.

JEANINE: But there must be some mistake. I didn't forward on any luggage.

CATHY: There is no mistake, Jeanine. May I call you Jeanine?

JEANINE (*Watching the driver exit with her luggage*): Yes, of course. I'd like that.

CATHY: I'll show you to your suite. You must be tired and want to rest now.

For no discernible reason, Henri Dusseau's anger has boiled up again, and he marches over to his wife and pushes her, before returning to his seat.

FRAU VON KESSEL: I demand to speak to the manager! You will call Herr Kaufmann and then you will offer an apology to me!

CATHY: Herr Kaufmann is dead.

FRAU VON KESSEL: Dead? How can he be dead? He was not even thirty years old when I first came here!

CATHY (*Turning away from her, a lovely smile on her face for Jeanine*): Shall we get started, Jeanine?

FRAU VON KESSEL (*Her arrogance giving way to sudden desperate fear*): You can't turn me away like this after all these years! I must have my rejuvenation treatment! Give me her room! Put her somewhere else! (*To Jeanine, opening her purse*) How much do you want? I'll buy your room.

CATHY: I can't allow you to buy someone else's room, Frau Von Kessel.

FRAU VON KESSEL: Why not? What difference does it make to you? (*To Jeanine*) Find another hotel. You're still young. You're still pretty.

CATHY: Please don't make a scene, Frau Von Kessel.

FRAU VON KESSEL (*To Jeanine in frightened desperation*): Please. Let me have your room. I'll . . . I'll share the room! I'll pay the entire bill and I'll share the room with you! It won't cost you anything! Everything will be free for you!

CATHY: You will have to leave now, Frau Von Kessel.

FRAU VON KESSEL (*Suddenly, viciously, turning on Jeanine*): It's all your fault, you miserable vindictive nobody!

JEANINE (*To Cathy*): Isn't here any space available for her? Couldn't you check your ledger again?

CATHY: If you wish. (*Looking at the reservation book*) Yes. There is one vacancy, but I'm sure it won't do.

FRAU VON KESSEL: Yes! It will do! I will take it!

CATHY: It's the room behind the kitchen.

There is a long pause as the effect of the humiliating suggestion registers on Frau Von Kessel's face.

I told you it won't do. Shall we go now, Jeanine?

FRAU VON KESSEL: I will take it! The smell of good cooking does not bother me.

CATHY: There is no window.

Another long pause.

FRAU VON KESSEL: I do not require a window. Sunlight is of no importance.

CATHY: There is no private bath. The bathroom must be shared with the kitchen staff.

FRAU VON KESSEL: I do not mind sharing the bath. Privacy is immaterial to me.

CATHY: As you wish. Please wait by the desk, Frau Von Kessel. Your room will be ready when the bell is rung. Shall we go now, Jeanine?

JEANINE (*To Frau Von Kessel with real compassion in her voice*): I'm sure they'll find better accommodations for you later in the week, Frau Von Kessel.

FRAU VON KESSEL (*Drawing herself up to her full haughty height, looking around and straight through Jeanine*): Did someone speak? I see no one.

Jeanine exits behind Cathy. Frau Von Kessel watches as Henri Dusseau walks over to his wife and stands over her, slowly striking the folded newspaper against his hand. Frau Von Kessel sits down on her suitcase, her cane between her legs, and stares at the silver bell on the desk. The rhythmic pounding of the newspaper against Henri Dusseau's palm has become frightening, menacing. Madame Dusseau shudders visibly at the sound of every blow. The lights begin to dim as Henri Dusseau whispers to his wife.

HENRI: Go! Go! Why don't you go?

Lights out. In the dark the voice of a young woman singing Franz Schubert's "Romanze," Opus 26, as we segue into Scene 3.

Scene 3

The great room of the Richelieu. The back wall is in shadowed darkness. Through what appears to be an enormous glass picture window can be seen the moonlit balustrade of the terrace and the deep snow-covered mountains beyond. Upstage center, directly in line with the distant mountains, is a sweet table laden with every imaginable after-dinner dessert: pastries with creams and rum, cakes and eclairs, chocolates and tarts, babas and amaretti, nuts, fruits, delicacies that spill from a wicker cornucopia, dark coffee from a silver urn, sweet liquors, brandies and iced champagne. At both ends of the sweet table, candles burn in multibranched silver candelabra. Midstage right and left are the alcoved entrances and exits of the room, the alcove at stage right mirrored, the alcove at stage left painted with a large mural of a hunting scene: horses and huntsmen, dogs attacking wild boar. Downstage, in the light of several heavy bronze floor lamps, a number of couches and chairs: heavy, dark pieces, upholstered, highbacked chairs with arms that end in claws. The room in its appointments seems medieval. For some moments the Schubert lied continues as the lights come up. A woman in her late forties, dressed in an elegant evening gown, sits alone. Judging from the soiled linen napkins, the leftover remains of drinks and desserts strewn about, the woman has had a number of companions who have eaten and gone. Listening now to the music, lost in her own thoughts, she seems unaware that the small demitasse cup has fallen from the saucer she still holds in her outstretched hand, and lies in broken shards on the floor. The music in the distant room stops. One of the two tuxedo-clad servants who has been cleaning up, disposing of the remains with the almost noiseless precision of the long practiced, jars her out of her revery as he softly sweeps the broken glass into a dustpan. It takes the woman some moments to regain her composure.

MRS. KARRAS: Could I have a little more coffee, Anthony?

ANTHONY: Certainly. (*Refilling her cup from a silver carafe and then returning to his cleaning*)

MRS. KARRAS: Do you know what piece that was they were playing?

ANTHONY: I'm afraid I don't, Mrs. Karras. Do you, Lester?

LESTER: Not likely. The wife says I have a tin ear.

MRS. KARRAS: It was nice. (*Sipping her coffee, glancing backward at the semidarkness of the room behind her, and then forward again*) It was all very nice.

Taking a final lingering sip of her coffee, Mrs. Karras starts to exit, pausing by the sweet table. She stares at the cornucopia, pouring forth its plenitude of fruit and nuts, and then picks up a kiwi fruit, turns it over, feeling its texture.

I always meant to try one of these. I used to see them all the time where I shopped. But they seemed so silly I passed them up for Anjou pears or apples. Whatever my husband liked or was on sale. (*Putting it back*)

ANTHONY: Would you care to take some with you now, Mrs. Karras? No trouble at all to wrap up a few.

MRS. KARRAS: No. I don't think so. (*Opening her purse and handing some bills to Anthony*) This is for you and Lester.

ANTHONY: Oh, there's no need for that, Mrs. Karras.

MRS. KARRAS: You've both been very thoughtful, and we can all use a little bit extra, especially with the holidays coming up.

ANTHONY: Thank you, Mrs. Karras.

MRS. KARRAS: Good night.

ANTHONY: Good night.

Mrs. Karras exits stage left, the two servants returning to their work.

LESTER: She's right about that. I've got to take the wife out next Sunday or she's going to have my head. Says she's tired seeing me sit in the house, my nose buried in the sports.

ANTHONY: Well, a man's got to satisfy his wife, now and then, or there's going to be no end to the grumbling, I suppose.

LESTER: That's the truth, all right. Damn kids coming down with the flu or the sniffles left and right and her stuck in the house all the time. Damn lack of privacy with the kids, if you know what I mean. Shut the bedroom door for a bit of privacy and you know what comes of it? Little knocks and scratching on the door. If a man's going to perform and keep turning out those little rug-rats, how's he supposed to do it with something like that going on?

ANTHONY: You should have gotten animals, instead. Wife and I put the cockerpoo out to stud and whelped enough to give us six weeks up at the lake.

LESTER: That a fact?

ANTHONY: She said to me right at the beginning, "Tony, hon, economic conditions being what they are, kids or cockerpoos? Let's flip and see what comes up." Never had a regret on that score. She's a smart one, my wife. Knows how to turn a situation into a profit.

LESTER: Mine can't even keep a crummy flower alive! Spent half a day's pay fixing an arboretum on the windowsill for her so she'd have something pretty . . . amaranthus, balsam, candy tuft. All she's got left now is a half-dead zinnia, its ugly little neck bent over and twisted looking for the sun!

ANTHONY: It's the dark that does 'em in. If you can't get the sun, you should look into the artificial. We got a bowl of silk poppy and metal nasturtium. Wife puts a drop of her Revlon into the ovary and they smell sweet as you please.

LESTER (*Looking over their handiwork: floor cleaned, tables cleaned, crumbs gone, fresh linen, neatly rowed silverware*): Clean as a whistle, wouldn't you say?

ANTHONY (*Studying the scene for a second*): Right as rain.

Sound of a woman's laughter. Jeanine and Dr. Atmos enter stage right. Both are in formal dress, as will be all the other guests of the Richelieu.

JEANINE (*Continuing to laugh in uneasy amusement*): I don't know where to begin.

DR. ATMOS: Why don't you begin at the end?

JEANINE: The end?

DR. ATMOS: Yes. The end when your husband decided he was finished with you and filed for divorce. Or the middle when you told me he stayed up all night staring at the fireplace rather than go upstairs and crawl into bed with you. It doesn't make any difference to me. I have the power to free you from your suffering no matter where you begin.

JEANINE (*Slightly lowering her voice in an attempt to get Dr. Atmos to do the same, his voice grown embarrassingly loud, the servants obviously overhearing*): Wouldn't it be more helpful if I began at the beginning, Dr. Atmos?

DR. ATMOS: Why? Do you think I am so anxious to hear again how you shattered your entire life in a single moment of carelessness?

JEANINE: Please, Dr. Atmos, not so loud.

DR. ATMOS: "Most fragile of all is the cherry-bloom, they say; but once my life was shattered at a single word." A Japanese gentleman, a Mr. Tsurauki, once told me that in strictest confidence, so you see you are not the only one who has had a life shattered in a single moment.

JEANINE: Please, Dr. Atmos!

DR. ATMOS: Mr. Atmos.

JEANINE: Mr. Atmos?

DR. ATMOS (*Looking at the dessert she has choosen*): Are you actually going to settle for that pathetically innocuous custard? Faced with the incredible splendor of the sweet table is that all you're going to eat? (*Abruptly turning to Anthony*) What is the cremolata flavored with this evening?

ANTHONY: Espresso, Doctor.

DR. ATMOS: Excellent. I'll have it.

JEANINE: I thought you were a doctor. Everybody at the table said you were a doctor.

DR. ATMOS: I am a doctor.

JEANINE: Then why is it "Mr. Atmos"?

DR. ATMOS: I didn't finish up. (*To Lester*) And a small slice of the pave au chocolat.

JEANINE: But if you didn't finish, how can you practice medicine? You need a license, don't you?

DR. ATMOS: Not all the time. Sometimes when you are out of the city you can practice medicine without a license. (*To Anthony*) Is that a charlotte russe? I haven't had a charlotte russe since I was sixteen. I must have it.

JEANINE: I have never heard of practicing medicine without a license.

DR. ATMOS: Have you ever heard of the tiny snail that lives all its life curled up quite contentedly in the gill flaps of the poisonous medusa jellyfish?

JEANINE: No.

DR. ATMOS: Well, there you have it! Believe me, Mrs. Cendrars, there are many strange things, odd facts, bizarre and inexplicable relationships in this world unheard of by most people. Foul, filthy, grotesque relationships.

The servants are having a hard time placing all of Dr. Atmos's desserts in his hands.

JEANINE: But if you don't have a degree in medicine, and you don't have a license, I really don't think I should be telling you all these things about myself.

DR. ATMOS: Why not? It's not costing you anything.

JEANINE: It could be harmful.

DR. ATMOS: What? Meaningless banter? Frivolous chitchat? (*Struggling with one arrangement after another of the desserts in his hands*)

JEANINE: They say even hypnosis can be dangerous in untrained hands.

DR. ATMOS: Oh, do they? Do they now? It just so happens it's not hypnosis that's dangerous in untrained hands, but the *love* of hypnosis. It's the same thing as money, you see. It's the *love* of money that's the root of all evil, not just money. Oh, there are some psychiatrists who have finished up all their work, doctors with impeccable credentials who have all their licenses, who still end up falling in love with hypnosis. They can't wait to hypnotize. But that is all to the detriment of the psychiatrist. It has nothing to do with the patient. The patient is never in any danger whatsoever.

JEANINE: I'm not sure I really agree with that, Dr. Atmos.

DR. ATMOS (*Suddenly blowing up as much from his frustration at being unable to discover a satisfactory arrangement that will allow him to carry all his desserts, as from Jeanine's bland comments*): Then don't agree with it! I have a list of clients waiting for my attention! Sick women whose husbands send them to me to be made well again! Sick women willing to undergo dangerous treatments in order to be healed: steaming salt vapors, electromagnetic impulse, drugs.

There is a slight disturbance at the stage-right entrance as Mimosa Klein enters, followed by Franco Boupacha. Dr. Atmos picks up as many of his desserts as he can handle and heads for a seat, Jeanine picking up the rest and joining him. Mimosa Klein is a tall, rather plain-looking, angular woman in her mid-thirties. She towers over her companion, a short, dark, oily, dangerous-looking individual, carrying her shawl.

MIMOSA: Get away from me, you miserable hound!

FRANCO (*Reaching up to pull a cigarette out of her lips*): You smoke too much.

MIMOSA: I will smoke as much as I please. (*Reaching in her purse for another cigarette*) I will drink as much as I please. I will do—

As soon as she puts the cigarette in her mouth, he pulls it out again.

I hate you! Do you know how much I hate you? (*Walking away from him and sitting down*)

FRANCO (*Following after with unflappable equanimity as always*): Put your shawl on. The room is chilly. (*When she makes no move to take the shawl, he places it around her*)

MIMOSA: Why don't you ask me who I was out with every night in Ottawa?

FRANCO (*Ignoring the provocation*): As soon as we've had some dessert, we'll retire for the night. We have to get an early start in the morning.

MIMOSA: I went out with a handsome distinguished gentleman a foot taller than you. (*Pauses, waiting for a response*) When he held me in his arms I could look up into his eyes. (*Pause*) I didn't have to bend my head down until my neck hurt. He took me out to the best restaurant. We wined and we dined and he made me laugh and I let him make love to me. It was beautiful. You hear that, you dwarf? You miserable, annihilating, suffocating dwarf! It was beautiful!

FRANCO: What dessert would you like?

MIMOSA: Do you know what making love is like when you don't have to look down at the top of a bald spot? When there is a canopy over the bed and the sheets are made of satin? When you are kissed by a man who doesn't walk around with a sweaty little upper lip like a Sicilian pimp?

FRANCO: What dessert do you want?

MIMOSA: Nothing! I am burning with the remembrance of all the men I have made love to behind your back!

FRANCO: (*To Anthony*): Madame will have something cool.

MIMOSA: I told you I don't want any dessert! Are you deaf as well as stupid?

FRANCO: Perhaps the pears in brandy . . . yes, they will do nicely.

Nodding his head at Anthony, who begins dishing them out.

MIMOSA: I don't want any dessert!

FRANCO: And put some of those delicious-looking brandied cherries in there as well for Madame.

MIMOSA: You disgust me! I have nothing but contempt for you!

FRANCO: And I will have a dish of the zuppa inglese . . . and a demitasse for two. (*Turning to Mimosa*) You do want a demitasse, or would you prefer the instant Maxwell House?

MIMOSA: You will pay for this!

FRANCO: Madame will have the demitasse.

MIMOSA (*As the desserts begin arriving*): When you die I will take your body to the taxidermist and have it stuffed! I will see to it that you are never buried!

Whispering furiously at Franco as he walks away and sits down on a nearby couch.

Moroccan dwarf!

Henri and Estelle Dusseau, unseen for the moment, enter arguing. The odd thing about arguments in public between the Dusseaus is that it is very hard to be absolutely sure that they are actually having an argument, since the angrier the words they utter the pleasanter the smile that filters them.

ESTELLE: I must talk to you! I can't go on this way!

HENRI: Then leave! There is the door! I will ring for the attendant to take your luggage!

Pausing for a moment at the edge of the stage-right alcove, the Dusseaus, aware others are in the room, become all smiles.

(*To Anthony*) Champagne.

ESTELLE: How cruel you are.

HENRI (*Snapping his fingers to bring the servant Lester hurrying to him*): Biscuit tortoni . . . mint. (*Handing Lester a crisp bill*)

ESTELLE (*As they enter the room, arm in arm*): Don't do this to me!

HENRI: I am bored with your jealousy! It no longer excites me! Do you understand? Leave me alone!

ESTELLE: You can't mean that! Please, Henri!

HENRI: Take your hands off me! You are making a public fool of yourself!

ESTELLE: I don't care! You can't leave me after twenty years of marriage. I won't be jealous anymore. I swear to you. I'm so much in love with you, Henri. Any woman who looks at you drives me crazy. I want to scratch her eyes out!

HENRI (*Grabbing her wrist*): Yes, you are a cat, and I will pull your claws out!

ESTELLE: Yes, pull my claws out . . . anything you want to do to me . . . anything! (*Rubbing her body against him, purring like a cat*)

The entire scene played out between Estelle and Henri is so personal and private that having to see and listen to it is a profound embarrassment to everyone else in the room. Each person tries to avoid hearing the humiliating public disclosures, witnessing the blatant sexual displays, in his own way.

Let me sip your champagne, Henri.

She begins sipping the champagne from his glass, and then she begins curling her tongue into it, licking it like a cat; and when some drops fall on his fingers, she licks his fingers. He watches her for a few moments.

HENRI: If you knew how much I have grown to despise these public displays . . . agh . . . here . . . take it!

Thrusting his champagne glass into her hands, Henri walks over to the other guests, leaving his wife to follow with the champagne and the desserts.

(*To Mimosa Klein and Franco Boupacha*) Permit me to introduce myself. I am Henri Dusseau. Dr. Atmos and Madame Cendrars I have already had the pleasure of chatting with at dinner.

FRANCO (*Rising and coming toward him, hand extended*): Franco Boupacha.

HENRI (*Shaking hands*): My pleasure. And you, charming lady?

MIMOSA (*Drawn to her feet as if magnetically compelled*): Mimosa Klein.

HENRI: Mimosa Klein? Not the Mimosa Klein who is a famous writer?

MIMOSA: Yes.

HENRI: But what an honor! Quel plaisir! I am thoroughly familiar with all your work . . . a great admirer. May I? (*Taking her hand and kissing it*) I must tell you how impressive I found your sixty-four short stories written at the mortuary temple of Ramses III at Medinet Habu. Exceptionnel! Absolument!

FRANCO: Mademoiselle Klein has always had an affinity for dead civilizations.

HENRI (*Staring into Mimosa Klein's eyes with all the intensity of some Romeo newly come upon some Juliet*): Incroyable! I myself also have this same affinity!

FRANCO (*Trying to insinuate himself between them*): In Egypt she doted over the remains of Pharaoh in his dirty winding sheet, the rotting rags wound round and round, the leather skin stiffening, until she felt faint in her white pilgrim underwear and had to be carried out of the vault.

HENRI: Fantastique!

He leads Mimosa Klein to the couch, Franco trailing.

FRANCO: Profond!

HENRI: Extraordinaire!

FRANCO: Miraculeux!

HENRI: Etonnant! (*Getting in the last compliment without ever taking his eyes off Mimosa Klein*)

As soon as Mimosa Klein sits down, Franco sits down beside her. Estelle Dusseau coughs. Jeanine is the only one who seems to be aware that Estelle Dusseau is just left standing by herself, ignored.

JEANINE: Aren't you going to introduce your wife, Monsieur Dusseau?

HENRI (*With a wave of his hand*): Yes. This is my wife.

ESTELLE (*Hastening over, her best social smile glued to her face, nodding her head slightly by way of greeting as she speaks*): I do hope the snowfall won't prevent us all from going on the midnight sleigh ride, Dr. Atmos. Henri and I have been so looking forward to it. (*Pointedly introducing herself to Mimosa Klein as she sits down beside her on the couch, taking the last available space*) Estelle Dusseau.

HENRI: (*Undaunted, casually positions himself in back of the couch, directly behind Mimosa Klein*): How extraordinaire to leave behind one's native shores to find the center of one's entire artistic expression in the haunting beauty of civilizations that can never fail our expectations.

MIMOSA (*Following him with her eyes, returning the depth and intensity of his gaze*): Yes. I've always had the feeling that life could be more than Newport in the summer and Boston in the winter.

Henri can't seem to prevent his fingers from touching her: a charmingly wayward strand of hair, the delicate lobe of her ear, her neck, the fabric of her dress. Each touch of his fingers tingles the nerve endings of Mimosa Klein; she struggles to maintain her ever-slipping decorum.

I suppose it's a rather terrible thing to admit, but by the time I was nineteen I was already suffering from what you French call "ennui," or as the Germans put it—and they're always so terribly precise about these things—"weltschmerz."

FRANCO (*Flicking one of Henri's fingers off Mimosa Klein's neck*): Mademoiselle Klein did an entire series of poems during her senior year at Wellesley on that subject. "In the Weltschmerz of My Nineteenth Year." (*Flicking another of Henri's fingers off Mimosa's arm*)

Henri, unable any longer to bear the physical separation from Mimosa, sits down on the arm of the couch next to his wife and begins to snake his body behind her toward Mimosa. The passion and desire that was only a moment before the merest brush of fingers has now become the full-fledged grope of hands.

MIMOSA: I can remember with such great precision the exact moment when this feeling of weltschmerz came upon me. I was reading T.S. Eliot and feeling very Christian. Father was in and out from Boston visiting Mother and me at Newport—we have a summer house there. He was just at that time recovering from his depression in the stock market—a depression he never failed to remind us that would have totally wiped him out had it not been for a fortuitous investment in radioactive waste disposal suggested to him by the Bishop of Boston . . .

Hands here, hands there, up an arm, down a leg, around a waist, below a breast; hands pulled off the knee by Madame Dusseau that reappear upon the arm; hands struck by the dessert spoon of Monsieur Boupacha that vanish from a shoulder only to snake around a waist. Estelle Dusseau struggles to hold onto her ever-shrinking beachhead on the couch, while all but Jeanine Cendrars gaily laugh, finding or pretending to find it all, conversation and event, terribly amusing.

. . . In return for this advice my father, the Rabbi Klein, totally accepted the Bishop of Boston as his personal savior, and had him out at least once a summer thereafter as our houseguest in Newport. To this day I can still see that poor man—he never had a chance to relax except when he was with us—sitting there by the side of the pool, his terribly white legs crossed in the water like cooked macaroni, talking away about theology and stock-market investments. Oooh!

Carried on the mounting wave of their cresting passion, Estelle Dusseau is unceremoniously dumped on the floor. For a moment there is stunned silence, and then it is all laughed away, none laughing more merrily than Estelle Dusseau.

JEANINE (*She alone upset*): Would you like to sit beside me, Mrs. Dusseau? This chair is empty. (*Gesturing toward the most impressive chair in the room, an almost thronelike chair*)

ESTELLE (*Picking herself off the floor and reseating herself on the edge of the couch*): No. Thank you. I am quite comfortable.

HENRI: Well, I am not comfortable! If you do not wish to sit there, I shall sit there! I will not have you crumpling up Mademoiselle Klein's evening gown!

ESTELLE (*To Mimosa Klein*): I am sorry.

HENRI: It is not enough to be sorry! It is necessary to move! (*When Estelle doesn't move fast enough*) Very well, then I will move! (*Making the slightest of efforts to rise*)

ESTELLE: No! No! I will move.

Estelle sits down next to Jeanine. For some moments silence hangs over all.

HENRI (*To Estelle*): Well, you see what you have done? You have poisoned the conversation!

Anthony has hastened over to change an ashtray because Mimosa Klein has lit a cigarette and flicked the merest hint of ash into it.

JEANINE (*To the servant*): Are there others coming do you know, or has all this dessert been set out for us?

ANTHONY: I believe Frau Von Kessel, Signorina Bottivicci and her cousin will be joining you, madame.

HENRI: Cesare Bottivicci, le grotesque?

ANTHONY: Yes, that's the gentleman, sir. (*Returning to the sweet table*)

HENRI: Charmant.

JEANINE: Le grotesque?

HENRI: I see you have not yet met Signorina Bottivicci's cousin, Mrs. Cendrars. Then you shall have the pleasure of experiencing a moment or two of the bizarre extraordinaire, le fabuleux, before the ultimate inanity of existence presses down upon us once again.

Frau Von Kessel, cane in hand, brocaded evening gown stiff as carapace, enters stage right.

Ah! Frau Von Kessel! (*Walking over to her at the sweet table*) What a pleasure to see you again. And how are you this evening?

FRAU VON KESSEL (*Staring at him for a moment*): I don't know you.

HENRI (*Clicking his heels and offering a slight bow*): Quite right. Henri Dusseau à votre service. We met briefly this morning just prior to your passing through the kitchen to your rooms.

FRAU VON KESSEL (*Silently ignoring the insult*): I don't know you. (*Turning to Anthony, behind the sweet table*) Bring something of everything to me. (*Brushing by Henri as if he were inanimate as a lamppost, she walks over to where Estelle is seated*) You are in my chair.

HENRI: Frau Von Kessel's husband was almost as famous as you, Mademoiselle Klein. He was in the steel business. A relative of the Krupps, I believe.

FRAU VON KESSEL: Are you going to be good enough to give me my chair?

HENRI: You are in Frau Von Kessel's chair, Estelle.

ESTELLE: I don't see why this is Frau Von Kessel's chair. We are all guests here.

HENRI: It is Frau Von Kessel's chair because it is the most comfortable chair. Frau Von Kessel always sits in the most comfortable chair. It doesn't matter where that chair is.

FRAU VON KESSEL (*Suddenly sticking her cane in Estelle's back*): You will oblige me!

As Estelle, intimidated, rises to her feet.

Alles verfault!

ESTELLE: I beg your pardon?

FRAU VON KESSEL: I said, "Everything degenerates!"

HENRI: Yes, of course it does.

Estelle shrinks off to a chair on the periphery of the group, half in half out of the shadows.

The Von Kessels have had the privilege of supplying armaments to the Fatherland for three wars. Unfortunately, since the factory was located in East Germany it was gutted by the Russians and transported back to Siberia, rolling stock and all. I believe it now produces bathroom fixtures and plumbing supplies, Herr Baron Von Kessel still in charge. The odd thing about it all is that with the Herr Baron in charge no matter what sort of bathroom fixture they produce it comes out looking like a field artillery piece. Très amusant, n'est-ce pas?

FRAU VON KESSEL: You will be still, or you will be sued for slander!

HENRI: I only repeat what is public knowledge, Frau Von Kessel.

FRAU VON KESSEL: My husband died in a Russian prison! A martyr for his beliefs!

HENRI: Absolument.

FRAU VON KESSEL: What are you? A filthy Bolshevik?

HENRI: I have no politics. I am apolitical.

FRAU VON KESSEL: A dissolute!

DR. ATMOS (*Calling out, without turning around, as if aware of the presence of Gabriella Bottivicci without seeing her*): Won't you join us, Signorina Bottivicci? (*For some moments no one steps forward out of the darkness*) Please come in! Come in!

And then a door in the stage-left mural seems to swing open by itself and Gabriella Bottivicci comes forward. She is as beautiful as her manner is shy and modest.

And where is you cousin? Won't he be joining us?

GABRIELLA: He was not feeling well earlier this evening.

DR. ATMOS: Ah, what a shame. Nothing serious, I hope.

GABRIELLA: No. He should be here shortly.

DR. ATMOS: Excellent. Excellent. Perhaps you will allow Monsieur Dusseau since he is already up to get you something from the sweet table?

HENRI: My pleasure.

GABRIELLA: No . . . please . . . don't bother . . . I am quite all right. (*Sitting down in a love seat*)

DR. ATMOS: Signorina Bottivicci and her cousin have just completed a triumphal tour of the continent and are now on their way to South America: São Paolo, Montevideo.

ESTELLE: Oh, how exciting! What sort of tour are you on, Signorina Bottivicci?

HENRI: Did you not hear the doctor say it was a triumphal tour?

Chided, Estelle pulls back into the shadows.

GABRIELLA: It is nothing really . . . a little magic show . . . auguries of the future.

DR. ATMOS: You are being far too modest. Signorina Bottivicci's cousin is a famous sensitive and clairvoyant. He has only to touch your hand and a thousand buried futures still undreamt will be exposed.

JEANINE: Is that true? Can your cousin really do that?

GABRIELLA: Some believe he can.

FRAU VON KESSEL: Claptrap!

GABRIELLA: If you wish.

JEANINE (*To Frau Von Kessel*): Oh, I don't see how anyone can know that for sure!

FRAU VON KESSEL: Did someone speak? I heard no one.

JEANINE: It could just as easily be that the future is always already there just waiting for us to notice it for the first time and be surprised.

DR. ATMOS: Yes, indeed . . . (*Looking directly at Jeanine and making her increasingly uncomfortable as he speaks*) like the tiny thread of a crack in the kitchen floor you step over without seeing a thousand times a day preparing your husband's meals, until one day something is said and the crack opens up between you like a chasm beneath your feet; or the tiny hole you notice for the very first time forming in the shower tile as you bathe, glistening above your head with a single bright bead of sea-green water like a child's eye looking back at you from another world.

HENRI (*Sitting down beside Gabriella*): Yes, I agree with Madame Cendrars. I wouldn't be so hasty forming a judgment, Frau Von Kessel. Signorina Bottivicci and her cousin have performed successfully before many heads of state and scientific bodies.

FRAU VON KESSEL: The world is filled with jackasses and fools who will believe anything.

MIMOSA: I support Monsieur Dusseau against you, Frau Von Kessel. Who's to say what we will all come to believe in at the end? An everlasting morning of resurrection, or an endless night in which we have grown old and wrinkled as turtles and hear nothing but the shoes of dead men walking endlessly about our bed?

FRAU VON KESSEL (*Gesturing furiously for Dr. Atmos to lean over*): Who is that woman?

DR. ATMOS: Mimosa Klein, Frau Von Kessel. I had the honor of introducing her to you in the dining room.

FRAU VON KESSEL: I don't remember seeing her.

DR. ATMOS: Perhaps she was hidden by the candlesticks. Mademoiselle Klein is a famous writer.

FRAU VON KESSEL: Nonsense! How can she be a famous writer when I have never heard of her?

DR. ATMOS: I don't know, Frau Von Kessel. Mademoiselle Klein's work is available at the checkout counter of every supermarket.

FRAU VON KESSEL: Alles verfault! The world degenerates until there is nothing left in it of the least consequence. (*Staring directly at Mimosa Klein*) Famous writers that no one of taste and position has ever read . . . (*Staring at Franco Boupacha*) dining-room tables presided over by Barbary apes with thickened lips and mottled teeth . . . savages who throw back their head to swallow a simple glass of wine, while the edge of a hoodlum's knife handle protrudes from their tuxedo!

Franco Boupacha, who has just, obligingly enough, tossed back his head to swallow his drink, belches.

FRANCO: Excuse.

Estelle walks over to the love seat and casually escorts Gabriella Bottivicci to another chair away from her husband as she speaks.

ESTELLE: I have always confined my reading to the best French authors: Dumas, Hugo, de Maupassant. I have found they are not nearly as troublesome as some of the others that are more frequently discussed: Flaubert, Stendhal, or the impossible Proust. With them I am always made to feel as if just when I am about to understand everything, everything just runs down the canvas of my mind like watercolor in rain. (*Returning to the love seat and sitting down beside her husband*)

HENRI (*Irritated*): What are you talking about?

ESTELLE: Just some famous French writers, mon cher. Frau Von Kessel was just—

HENRI: What do you know about famous French writers? Eh? Eh? What do you know? (*Pause*) Are you trying to embarrass me?

ESTELLE: Of course not, mon cher.

HENRI: Then why do you go on and on talking about nothing you understand? Have I ever required anything more of you than to keep the furniture dusted and the house in order? (*Walking away from her over to the sweet table to get another drink*)

JEANINE (*Coming to Estelle Dusseau's rescue after a long humiliating pause*): My husband and I purchased a nineteenth-century farm house outside of Sewickley, Pennsylvania, and I did most of the restoration myself. I didn't think I could, but it turned out I could do a little bit of everything.

ESTELLE: Yes. I can do a little bit of everything . . . also.

DR. ATMOS: You two ladies mustn't denigrate your accomplishments. We are all under a moral imperative to shine forth and radiate.

ESTELLE: Not everyone can do that, Dr. Atmos.

DR. ATMOS: So you envy those that do, eh?

JEANINE: I think all Madame Dusseau meant was that some of us are never going to shine forth.

DR. ATMOS: Not like Miss Klein and Signorina Bottivicci, eh? You recognize their accomplishments and wish you could be like them, is that not so?

JEANINE: I don't know. I . . .

MIMOSA: Really, Dr. Atmos, I must protest. Although there is undoubtedly some truth in what you say, it's somewhat embarrassing being held up as an object of envy for others.

DR. ATMOS: But you are, and you know it, dear lady! Allow us to give homage where homage is due! People such as yourself radiate like glowing clouds of Magellanic gas across the night sky. You attract, even without meaning to, lesser creatures who flock about like so many hapless moons shining in reflected light. I'm sure Mr. Boupacha will bear me out on that. By the way, that is a knife you have thrust there under your tuxedo, isn't it, Mr. Boupacha?

FRANCO: And what if it is? (*Taking the knife out and menacingly approaching Dr. Atmos with it*)

DR. ATMOS (*With mounting nervousness*): Nothing. Dear me, nothing at all. Just making idle conversation, chitchat.

FRANCO: You are interested in knives?

DR. ATMOS: Not at all . . . only from a medical point of view . . . dissection scalpels . . . tools of the trade . . . that sort of thing.

FRANCO (*Placing the knife against Dr. Atmos's throat*): My knife is as sharp as a scalpel. Sometimes I have occasion to use it to perform surgery.

DR. ATMOS: I imagine you do.

FRANCO: Slicing off the skin of an apple, the yellow fat under the throat of a goose.

MIMOSA: Enough!

FRANCO: Some prefer chitchat. I, myself, prefer the knife. A man brushes up against me in a cafe—there is my knife; a chance remark others might not take as an insult is uttered—there is my knife; a woman I desire in passing resists—there is my knife, the blade cold on the trembling surface of her belly.

MIMOSA: I said enough! You are at the Richelieu, not some foul sink-hole stinking of Cointreau and moussaka!

FRANCO: Absolument! (*Putting the knife away, smiling, the menace evaporated as if it had been nothing more than a moment's diversion, a jest*)

DR. ATMOS (*Clapping his hands, laughing with the others, the jest accepted*): More sweets! More champagne!

The servants come forward with trays of champagne.

ESTELLE (*Rising to her feet*): Perhaps I will have just one more glass of champagne. (*As she takes a glass*) Is that all right, Henri?

HENRI: Take what you want.

ESTELLE: I only had a glass or two in the dining room. (*To the others*) Henri is such a good judge of how much I can have to drink.

HENRI (*Suddenly exasperated*): I said take as much as you want!

Estelle smiles faintly, and then lowers her head and walks back to her seat.

JEANINE (*To Gabriella*): How long have you and your cousin been touring, signorina?

GABRIELLA: Three months. We will spend another three months in South America and then return to Ravenna in the spring.

JEANINE: That is your home?

GABRIELLA: Yes. Cesare and I were born there, as have all the members of our family.

JEANINE: It must be wonderful having a place that's always there for you. You must find it difficult to leave.

DR. ATMOS: Signorina Bottivicci and her cousin have been inseparable since childhood. When it was necessary for him to leave their sadly debilitated estate to earn a buck, she could not imagine remaining behind.

GABRIELLA: And you, signora, do you travel with someone?

JEANINE: I'm alone.

DR. ATMOS: Madame Cendrars has hopes that her husband will be joining her, since her luggage was mysteriously forwarded on without her knowledge.

GABRIELLA: How strange.

DR. ATMOS: Yes.

HENRI (*Going over and taking Gabriella's hand*): Perhaps the signorina will tell us what gods she tempts with her psychic powers? Can you also tell a man's fate by the touch of his hand?

GABRIELLA (*Gently withdrawing her hand*): I'm afraid, Monsieur Dusseau, my powers are only to see to it that my cousin is presented to the world in his most perfect appearance: the cusp of his handkerchief arranged just so in his breast pocket, the cuticles of his nails pushed back to perfect translucent arcs, the polish of his shoes done to such a shine the stagelights seem moons in a lacquered pool. . . . All attended to that he may shine.

DR. ATMOS: And this is sufficient for you, Signorina Bottivicci? You do not perhaps envy your cousin his powers?

GABRIELLA: To envy another, even one as close to me as Cesare, I would have to believe that in me God placed an unfulfilled promise: an ovary without eggs, a dawn without light. There is no such unfulfilled promise in me.

DR. ATMOS: Well said. (*Without turning his head, calling out to someone unseen*) Wouldn't you say so, Signor Bottivicci? (*Pause*) Come in! Come in! You must join us.

Again the door in the mural mysteriously swings open. When Cesare Bottivicci comes into the light his appearance causes an immediate shock among the guests who have not yet seen him. Cesare, dressed exactly as described by Gabriella, has the face of a beast!

CESARE (*Standing there for some moments as the shock of his appearance dies down*): Forgive me for not dining with you. I was not feeling well.

DR. ATMOS: Signor Bottivicci's disfigurement often causes him great discomfort and pain. (*Gesturing for Cesare to fully come out of the alcove and enter the room*) Please, come in, make yourself comfortable. Signorina Bottivicci was just telling us how happy she is traveling about with you, making herself as useful as possible in the service of your gifts.

CESARE (*Entering*): What poor gifts I have we are both in service to, Dr. Atmos. As for happiness, it is she who has brought happiness to me. That I have not completely withdrawn from the world I owe entirely to my dear Gabriella. (*Reaching out and clasping his cousin's hand*) She found me in the labyrinths of a dark garden and brought me out to where there was light.

ESTELLE: What a charmingly romantic thing to say!

JEANINE: If I ever found a place I loved I would put a wall around it . . . keep it forever as it was . . . let nothing change it.

CESARE: Would that that were possible, signora. I have often in my thoughts cast my mind's eye back to that first walled place, that first labyrinthine garden of God's, and saw there only a vision of limitless horror: in the morning the sun moving across the sky in a clear voyage of light, the mists just rising from the just-created rainy wildernesses. On the savannas the lions all formed, parading; the zebras whinnying, striking the excellence of earth. God's glass bowl of time held over the earth as if glass might keep a season cloudy-fair forever, save the innocent from malice and betrayal. And then the afternoon comes moving through the mind of God. The glass lifts from the globe of earth as easily as a child might lift the bowl of a terrarium. The zebras sense it in the breath that blows the hot swarms of gathering flies; the wildebeest, circling, starting, a buzzing premonition low upon them . . . the ibex . . . all the trusting innocent. In multitudinous hurt the afternoon explodes: monkeys the color of penny-red firecrackers pop in the mouths of snakes uncurling in the baobab trees, the cricket in the lizard's mouth rubs its legs in song a final time, the ibex down in the wet idyllic grass, stunned and stunned again by the blooded paw, while flies arrive at their own special moment of truth—licking the still open wonder of a zebra's eye!

ESTELLE: Oh . . . !

CESARE (*To Jeanine*): It is always that way with the things we love, signora, for all things wish to remain unbetrayed in their perfection, eternal in the bright flag of their beauty. But God will not have it so. What we do not leave, leaves us. What we do not betray, betrays us. He will have it no other way. (*Sitting down beside his cousin*)

DR. ATMOS: Come, come, Signor Bottivicci, continue on in this way and you will sour the whipped cream in Madame Cendrars' custard, or at the very least put Frau Von Kessel to sleep. It's hardly God's fault each of us must end his existence nourishing pâté in the mouth of the other.

ESTELLE: Oh . . .!

FRAU VON KESSEL (*Suddenly, angrily pointing her cane at Cesare Bottivicci*): Is that his true face, or is it some mask he has put on?

CESARE: It is my true face, signora. I have no other.

GABRIELLA: The signora may find the appearance of my cousin somewhat unsettling, but I can assure her it is his true face that she sees, and that he is as incapable of speaking deceit as he is altering what he is. Therefore, I warn you be careful in what you ask of him.

FRAU VON KESSEL: Ask of him? I ask nothing of him! I was merely startled to see such grotesquery!

CESARE: Being unable to resist what I am, I have sought to find God in what I am.

HENRI: You must excuse Frau Von Kessel, Signor Bottivicci. Since losing her husband, the Herr Baron, in the war, happiness has been alien to her. Is that not so, Frau Von Kessel?

FRAU VON KESSEL: I wish you to mind your own business, do you understand?

HENRI: Absolument.

FRAU VON KESSEL: To listen to miserable little insects such as yourself discussing the great is intolerable!

HENRI: The great?

FRAU VON KESSEL: Yes! The great ones of this world! The ones who controlled the political destiny of nations! Men like my husband, the Herr Baron. Giants whose widows you now think you can insult with impunity because they are no longer alive to protect us! I tell you better the bloodlines of this wretchedly deformed creature than a world filled with popinjays and petty functionaries such as yourself!

HENRI: Really, Frau Von Kessel, it is not necessary to insult Signor Bottivicci in order to insult me. (*Draining his glass of champagne*) I am quite prepared to be insulted on my own. In fact I insist on it. (*Gesturing to one of the servants for a refill*)

FRAU VON KESSEL: Dissolute! (*Rising to her feet, calling out to the servants at the sweet table*) You have not given me everything I have asked for! The cherries brandied with flame, marzipan, pudding, champagne! (*Whirling about and pointing her cane at Cesare again*) If that man is not a complete and utter fraud like everything else that has remained in this world, let him show me his power! Let him show me the future dancing in the palm of a hand! (*Taking a few steps toward Cesare, who has grown increasingly distressed by her remarks*) According to her you have only to touch another's skin to see the future . . . (*Holding out her hand*) then touch my skin. (*Imperiously*) Touch my skin, Herr Charlatan, and tell me what future you see inside of me!

Goaded by her unrelenting command, Cesare rises, walks over, and suddenly covers Frau Von Kessel's face with his hand. As soon as his hand touches her face, Frau Von Kessel audibly gasps. Throughout the "reading" she writhes in great and obvious pain.

CESARE: A wind sharper than a man's knife to peel away your skin . . . flayed skin like leather . . . strip by strip. The wind that blows like sand, abrading, dissolving, eating away organ by organ, sliver by sliver, until only the dust of the mold in which you were formed remains . . . dust free of all pain, desire. Lady of Flayed Skin.

Suddenly, with a shriek, Frau Von Kessel collapses to the floor. Dr. Atmos and the servants run to her assistance, lifting her under the arms, pulling her back to her chair. Frau Von Kessel screams at Cesare as he returns to his seat beside his cousin. But her speech now seems momentarily slurred as if she has suffered some kind of stroke.

FRAU VON KESSEL: Fraud! Charlatan! You pretend to see the future, but all you see are the natural effects of the restorative treatments I am undergoing. The tissues being regenerated, the smoothness of the texture from the injections of lamb embryo and royal jelly. Is that not so, Dr. Atmos?

DR. ATMOS (*Kneeling beside her*): Absolutely. You grow more beautiful every year, Frau Von Kessel. You are the envy of all your friends.

FRAU VON KESSEL (*To Dr. Atmos*): Sweets! More sweets! More cherries! More brandy!

As Frau Von Kessel lies sprawled back in her chair, unable even to sit up straight, one of the servants spreads a large napkin across her chest and Dr. Atmos begins spooning brandied cherries into her mouth. Frau Von Kessel spits the pits out onto a little plate held by the servant. As the feeding proceeds, Estelle Dusseau walks over to Cesare.

ESTELLE: What do you make of me, Signor Bottivicci?

HENRI: For the love of God.

ESTELLE: I want to know what he sees! It's important to me! (*To Cesare*) Tell me what you see. Please!

Cesare hesitates for a moment, and then holds out his arm, his open fingers forming a rigid cup into which Estelle Dusseau places her face.

CESARE: Rings of emerald and aquamarine, diamond chips and pearl. Lady so careful in her dressing . . . the filed and coated nails, rows of powders, vials and stoppered flasks with swans of glass . . . brushed cheeks and appliqués of lipstick, blotted and applied again . . . lotioned hands wrung round and round the livered spots, the tear that stains through dark mascara . . . false lashes float where false dreams fade.

Estelle Dusseau, in tears and pain, backs away as Cesare, looking directly at her now, continues speaking.

The lady sits in the arc of beauty's light and sees the darkness beyond, wondering if it will have any pity for her . . . Lady of Many Ornaments who has outlived her usefulness.

Estelle Dusseau sways on her feet, almost collapsing. Franco Boupacha hastens over, catching her in his arms.

FRANCO: Are you all right, Madame Dusseau?

HENRI (*Walking over*): Of course she's all right. She's just had too much to drink. Isn't that so?

ESTELLE: Yes. My husband is quite correct. Thank you so much, Monsieur Boupacha. Très galant.

To the others, as Franco Boupacha sits down.

Very silly of me. I felt dizzy for a moment and thought I was going to fall. But I quite enjoyed what Signor Bottivicci had to say. I found it quite . . . amusing. Really. (*Going over to the sweet table*) I think I will have a little dessert after all.

CESARE (*Noticing that Mimosa Klein has been staring fixedly at him, he rises to his feet*): Perhaps it would be best if I withdraw from the room.

MIMOSA: Please. No. I'm sorry. I didn't mean for you to infer that at all.

CESARE: I have no wish to cause the signorina any distress. I know my presence fills many people with disgust.

MIMOSA: No. You do not upset me. It's just something. . . . In looking at you I was reminded of something else.

FRANCO: You must remain, Signor Bottivicci. Be seated . . . please.

Cesare sits down again.

And be assured Miss Klein means what she says. There is room for only one beast in her life, and I have the honor of vying for that position.

MIMOSA: Be still for once!

FRANCO (*To Mimosa*): Perhaps you ought to tell Signor Bottivicci exactly what it is you are reminded of in looking at him. (*When she doesn't respond*) You see, Signor Bottivicci, Mademoiselle Klein is haunted by the image of a centaur she once saw in, of all things, a child's comic book given to her when she was seven or eight years old. Somehow this image became linked in Mademoiselle's mind with the very wellsprings of her creative genius. Although, of course, she didn't realize it at the moment, for the rest of her life she would look back on the image of that pale blue cheaply inked creature of fancy in a comic book and know it to be the exact moment when her spirit became charged with the unshakeable knowledge of truth and beauty, that dazzling moment when the artist that was to be Mimosa Klein first picked up her weapons to wage war against the chaos of the universe. And so, now and then, when Mademoiselle is not totally tied up with her literary endeavors, she has me search out for her dealers of antique comic books . . . searching in a wilderness of infantine memorabilia for a single pale blue cheaply inked centaur. Of such grotesque stuff is true genius made! With such a grotesque beast am I in battle for the sole possession of the heart of Mimosa Klein! Incredible!

GABRIELLA: Perhaps not, Signor Boupacha. All our lives are made up of tiny unremembered flashes that have gleamed and dimmed so quickly we fail to put a name to them. It is a wonder that Mademoiselle Klein has managed to make so much of her moment. She is to be applauded, though I don't believe that was your intent.

FRANCO (*Walking over to the sweet table*): I assure you, signorina, I only mention these things to amuse.

GABRIELLA: To betray.

FRANCO (*Looking at the sweet table, spinning the chocolates around on their rotating platter*): You see how everything pours forth in endless abundance: the chocolates dancing in their silver coats, the whirls and curlicues of pastry, the apple strudel ripe and bulging with plump nuts and raisins, like Mimosa Klein's literary genius, life's bountiful surplus in swollen splendor. (*To Anthony*) Is the nasprata filled with custard or ricotta?

ANTHONY: Ricotta.

FRANCO: Excellent. Just as it should be. Mademoiselle Klein will have the nasprata, and I another portion of the zuppa inglese.

MIMOSA: I do not wish dessert! (*Standing up and starting to exit*)

FRANCO (*Hastening over with her dessert, blocking her exit*): You must try some of this.

He holds the dessert out to her. When she refuses to take it, he scoops out a spoonful and holds it out for her to eat off the spoon.

You really must!

For some long moments she remains motionless, the two of them frozen in a tableau, and then she takes the spoon out of his hand and flicks the dessert on the white front of his tuxedo. No one speaks in the shocked silence. The dessert runs down the front of Franco Boupacha's shirt. His voice when he speaks now is full of contrition.

I have behaved like a beast. You must accept my apology.

MIMOSA: You make me sick! There's not one inch of true feeling inside of you. Why must you endlessly pretend there is?

FRANCO: You see how it is, dear ladies? I, the gentle artist of the knife, must repress all my natural feelings in order to be of service to this lady.

MIMOSA: You have no feelings.

FRANCO: My gifts for compassion and delicate—

MIMOSA: You have no gifts.

FRANCO: Then you must accept my apology. (*Casually scooping up another spoonful of dessert and holding it in front of her lips, his voice taking on a sudden domineering edge again*) You must!

After a moment, Mimosa opens her mouth and allows the spoonful of dessert to be slid in. There is an audible release of tension in the room: a hundred quirks and motions suspended without thought begin again.

DR. ATMOS: You see, Monsieur Boupacha, you are forgiven. The clouds have blown away and all again is sunshine.

HENRI (*Getting to his feet and heading over to the sweet table for another drink*): Hardly worth the effort to have even raised a fuss.

DR. ATMOS (*Continuing, after giving Henri a momentary glance, weighing his derisive comment*): I think we always tend to place an undue amount of importance on these little quarrels we have between ourselves. They are really of no greater significance than a fingernail of cloud across the sun.

HENRI: Death, too, n'est-ce pas, dear doctor? A moment or two digging one's fingernails into the white sheet of a hospital bed or the soft frayed arm of a chair and that, too, is finished with.

DR. ATMOS: Death? Who said anything about death? Why talk about such unpleasant things, Monsieur Dusseau? The night is alive with charming companions, the candles burn brightly as ever, the sweet table still filled to overflowing.

HENRI (*Gesturing for Anthony to fill his outstretched champagne glass*): I think some recognition is in order to Dr. Atmos who sees to it that all the guests of the Richelieu move along at their proper pace like viscous knots of undigested food in the bowels. (*Raising his glass*) To Dr. Atmos who sees us as we truly are: eyes to weep, holes to eat, stomach gas to keep us fully awake so we don't miss a single awe-inspiring moment of our stupidly brief and transitory tumble through the cosmos, while the dandruff falls, the arches fall, the saggy breasts of time decline to point their nipples upward.

He drinks the champagne and then holds out his glass for a refill. Anthony pauses, looking at Dr. Atmos for permission. Dr. Atmos gives an almost imperceptible nod, and the glass is filled.

And to all of us, as well, without whom Dr. Atmos would find himself bored to death: ladies and gentlemen who dance about with stupid pathological conditions, stupid cancerous changes, battling to the very end the poisonous infamy of microbes, stupid atom hanging onto stupid atom for dear life, stupid cell to stupid cell with all the terrible tenacity of our stupid lives until the maid comes in to turn the covers down and then—why, good night!

FRAU VON KESSEL (*Quite recovered now, angrily striking her cane against the floor*): Oh, do stop that, you irritating, annoying man! We are trying to let our stomachs settle with some sweets, not have you go on and on this way!

HENRI (*Swallowing his drink*): I apologize. How stupid of me.

DR. ATMOS: Frau Von Kessel does have a point, Monsieur Dusseau. It is not necessary to mock everything.

HENRI: I only mock the ultimate faithless villainy of this world, dear doctor. It is far worse than anything Signor Bottivicci has envisioned.

JEANINE: But how could it be worse, Monsieur Dusseau?

HENRI: It is worse, charming lady, because it is happening to me! Existence that comes to whisper immortality in my ear, then eats my flesh and wipes the blackened corner of its mouth like the cheating slut it is! The violet eyes of a hundred women met by chance upon some boulevard that fix upon me with all the expectations of my pounding heart, then vanish irretrievably in the checkered shade beyond the elms! Delusions and more delusions! A coating of stars smeared across a heaven of blackest pitch!

Seeking to rest his hand on the arm of a chair, Henri, somewhat drunk, misses, and tumbles to the floor.

DR. ATMOS (*Coming to his aid, helping him up*): You mustn't take it all so personally, my friend.

Estelle leads her husband over to the love seat.

ESTELLE: Henri cannot imagine how a universe that is personally faithless to him—thinning his hair . . . causing him periodontal pain—can be faithful to anyone else.

FRAU VON KESSEL: I wonder where Monsieur Dusseau has even found such thoughts.

ESTELLE: Henri tends to see the world through his own heart. His sensitivity causes him a great deal of suffering.

FRAU VON KESSEL: Perhaps he has been seated by mistake in the first-class compartment of some train and has overheard the conversations of his betters.

HENRI: Or perhaps I am merely like you, Frau Baron—nothing left but my outrage and my stupidities.

FRAU VON KESSEL: You are not like me at all! People like you exist to place parcels on a scale, lick the mucilage of stamps!

DR. ATMOS (*After a moment of silence*): Well, well, what is it all anyway? Banter, chitchat, a bit of persiflage with a good meal in our belly, a taste of sweetness pouring out of a wicker cornucopia while it lasts. I, for one, have enjoyed myself immensely, and if I could persuade the one guest who has so far remained quite within herself to join in these little festivities, I should count the entire evening an enormous success. (*Staring around the room from one to another like a schoolteacher seeking an unprepared pupil, and then pouncing*) Won't you join in, Mrs. Cendrars?

JEANINE (*Smiling uncomfortably*): I'm just enjoying myself listening.

DR. ATMOS: But you've been listening all evening. Surely there is something you would like to say.

JEANINE (*Walking over to the sweet table*): I was thinking of trying some of the chocolate cake. Everything is so wonderful, I didn't know what to try.

FRANCO: I can recommend the zuppa inglese . . . the brandied cherries.

MIMOSA: The nasprata.

HENRI: Frau Von Kessel can recommend the entire sweet table; she's eaten it all.

FRAU VON KESSEL: Come over here and I will give you all the sweet poison you want from my tongue! (*Sticking out her tongue and flicking it provocatively*)

DR. ATMOS (*To Anthony*): Pave au chocolat for Madame. (*To Jeanine*) And some champagne, perhaps?

Jeanine nods.

Yes. Champagne. (*To Anthony*) Perrier Jouet.

To the others, as Jeanine returns to her seat.

Mrs. Cendrars and her husband came to the Richelieu some years ago on their honeymoon.

ESTELLE: What a wonderful place to come to for a honeymoon!

GABRIELLA: Your husband is going to join you here, later?

JEANINE (*Beginning to appear visibly uneasy*): I don't know. I'm not sure.

DR. ATMOS: Mrs. Cendars hopes her husband will be joining her later since he forwarded on her luggage to the hotel, but the significance of this is uncertain since he is also in the process of suing her for a divorce.

GABRIELLA: Oh . . . I'm sorry.

MIMOSA: No chance the marriage could be saved?

FRAU VON KESSEL: Any woman can save her marriage if she plays her cards right in the bedroom.

MIMOSA: Actually this reminds me of an absolutely fascinating parallel situation I came across while researching my Pulitzer Prize-winning novel on Henry II and Eleanor of Aquitaine. It seems she, too, was constantly being threatened with divorce by her husband, moved about from one castle to the other, but she never let him get away with it. Of course, they had any number of children, and what with the problems of succession to the throne, the machinations of the court and the religious difficulties being caused by Thomas à Becket, I don't suppose the situations are alike at all. In any event the novel actually won the National Book Award as well.

A gay round of applause by all over Mimosa Klein's good fortune.

ESTELLE: We won't have any trouble hearing the sleighs when they're brought around, will we, Dr. Atmos? Henri and I have been so looking forward to the ride through the forest.

DR. ATMOS: No trouble at all, Madame Dusseau.

MIMOSA: The divorce must have come as a shock to you.

JEANINE: No. I had been expecting it.

DR. ATMOS: The possibility of divorce hung over the marriage for a number of years like a knife.

ESTELLE (*Glancing at her husband as she speaks*): Living in dread of something is the worst fear. It's better to crawl on all fours toward the guillotine and have it done with.

GABRIELLA: I don't think we ought to be discussing Mrs. Cendrars' divorce.

DR. ATMOS: It's just chitchat, persiflage.

ESTELLE: In any event we're all sure it wasn't Mrs. Cendrars' fault.

DR. ATMOS: Actually it was.

JEANINE: Please . . .

DR. ATMOS: I don't think I would be violating Mrs. Cendrars' confidence if I told you the divorce was precipitated by the death of their only child.

Anthony hands Jeanine her cake and champagne.

JEANINE: Please! What I told you was in the strictest confidence, Dr. Atmos!

DR. ATMOS: Mr. Atmos. I did everything but the final work. (*Turning to the others*) What happened was that Mrs. Cendrars and her husband, an aspirant for public office, were ferrying over the Saguenay, Mrs. Cendrars holding their child in her arms. It was one of those rare warm spring days you so seldom see in southern Quebec, the wind softly lifting her hair. When she saw her husband getting ready to take her picture, she put the child down. She was so much in love, so busy primping and posing for her husband, she forgot all about the child!

Jeanine leaps to her feet at the accusation and begins to walk falteringly toward Dr. Atmos.

The child, of course, scampered through the open chain railing and vanished totally into the churning foam. It was only a matter of a moment, but since when did it ever take more than a moment to shatter anyone's life.

As the final accusatory blow is delivered, Jeanine's arm goes limp and the cake slides off her plate onto the floor. She stands motionless, unaware that it has even fallen.

At the present time Mrs. Cendrars is doing her very best to hold herself together through the long months of painful court procedure. Property must be divided, her pleas for reconciliation ignored, the horrendous burden of blame assigned.

Franco picks the fallen cake off the floor, places it back on the plate, and licks the chocolate off his fingers.

MIMOSA (*To Franco*): Oh, don't be quite such an imbecile! She's not going to eat the cake once it's fallen to the floor!

DR. ATMOS (*Taking the plate and champagne glass out of Jeanine's hands and setting them down, as she rigidly stands there, lost in her own thoughts*): I'm sure you have the deepest sympathy of everyone here on your loss, Mrs. Cendrars. May I call you Jeanine?

ESTELLE: Yes, she has mine.

DR. ATMOS (*To the servants*): Another pave au chocolat for Mrs. Cendrars!

MIMOSA: Though I've never had a child I can imagine what the loss of a child must feel like. As a matter of fact, artistically speaking, I can feel the loss with greater anguish than most people who have actually been through it.

FRAU VON KESSEL: When they took my Baron away, everything sweet went out of my life. Every lick of summer sherbet seared the roof of my mouth. (*To the servants*) Bring me macaroons! Bring me cremolata!

JEANINE: The curve of his body still rests in my arms; my fingers are the mold of his neck and skull.

Sound of sleigh bells approaching.

DR. ATMOS (*Clapping his hands*): Ah, the sleighs! The sleighs we've all been waiting for are here, ladies and gentlemen! (*With all the enthusiasm of a circus ringmaster*) Babylon or Fez, Ankara or Nineveh, I tell you my friends, when I hear the sound of the sleighs of the Richelieu coming about, I would willingly trade all my days in sunny lands for one midnight ride through the boreal forest, the ice crystals shrouding the horses' nostrils like foggy puffs of blue diamond dust. (*Rubbing his hands*) Ah, that's the spice that rejuvenates!

Jeanine addresses her comments from one to the other; but, with the exception of Cesare and Gabriella, they all seem to have lost interest, caught up now in the impending sleigh ride offered by Dr. Atmos.

JEANINE: When I try to sleep at night, I feel the imprint of his body beside me on the pillow. I listen to his sweet soft breathing. I am not sure whether I am a ghost in his life or he is a ghost in mine.

Cesare, moved by his compassion, goes over to her, touches her hand to console her, and then as if confirming what he felt, places his hand on her cheek for some moments. When he takes his hand away, it is obvious from the expression on his face that he has been strongly affected. Only Dr. Atmos seems to have noticed; the others, moving about, are too involved in getting themselves ready to leave.

DR. ATMOS: Is there something wrong, Signor Bottivicci?

CESARE: No. Nothing.

DR. ATMOS (*Pursuing the matter with an almost detective-like curiosity*): You seemed surprised.

CESARE: I am always surprised.

Dr. Atmos stares quizzically at Cesare for some moments, until the desk clerk, Cathy, briefly enters.

CATHY (*Announcing*): The sleighs! The sleighs are here, ladies and gentlemen! (*Exits*)

FRAU VON KESSEL (*Standing*): I wish to ride alone. Do you have a separate sleigh for me?

DR. ATMOS: Of course, Frau Von Kessel.

FRAU VON KESSEL: Then you will be kind enough to escort me to it.

DR. ATMOS: (*Hesitating for a moment between his desire to question Cesare further and giving his full attention to Frau Von Kessel. Curiosity gives way to courtesy*) My pleasure as always, Frau Von Kessel.

FRAU VON KESSEL: My furs! I cannot go without my furs!

Dr. Atmos: Your furs are already waiting for you at the door, Frau Von Kessel.

FRAU VON KESSEL: Good! Good! (*Exiting*)

ANTHONY AND LESTER: Your macaroons, Frau Von Kessel! Your cremolata! *(Running after the departed Frau Von Kessel, desserts in hand)*

MIMOSA: *(To Franco, suddenly deciding not to let Frau Von Kessel get ahead of her):* Come! I want to be in the lead sleigh so everything will be seen new, the snow unbroken in front of me.

She exits with Franco, trying to catch up to Frau Von Kessel.

HENRI: (*Calling out to Dr. Atmos as he is about to exit*): And if one does not wish to stumble about in the snow? If one wishes something more personalized, more suitable to his unique and individual tastes than being paraded about the ice in a communal display of silk scarfs and dinner jackets?

DR. ATMOS: What that something more might be I cannot even imagine, Monsieur Dusseau. The sleigh ride has always been the traditional end to the evening at the Richelieu. (*Exits*)

HENRI (*Shouting after him*): Well, I can imagine it! I do not have any trouble imagining all the things that are being withheld! All that one is forever being led to expect at the Richelieu that does not occur!

ESTELLE (*Walking over to Henri after some moments of silence*): Henri insisted I bring along only my best clothes. He felt I wouldn't feel comfortable at the Richelieu with anything less. Didn't you, Henri?

HENRI (*Still preoccupied by his exchange with Dr. Atmos*): Didn't I what?

ESTELLE: Insist that I bring along all my best clothes.

HENRI: I don't know what you're talking about.

ESTELLE: Henri can never seem to decide which of the furs he has bought me complements my complexion best in the moonlight. (*Slipping her arm through his*) Which fur would you like to see me wear out this evening, mon amour? The silver fox? The lynx?

HENRI: Wear whatever you like! It is of no concern to me! (*As they exit*) Must you dig your nails into my skin? Is it never enough for you to just hold on?

Cesare and his cousin start to exit after Henri and Estelle.

JEANINE (*To Cesare*): Won't you tell me what you saw?

Cesare turns and silently looks at her for a moment.

Is there something still more painful to come to me?

CESARE: Only the unending pain of your hope. The hope you will not abandon for all the things that will not be.

JEANINE: I have hope . . . yes. Like your cricket rubbing its legs a final time in the lizard's mouth . . . I have that hope.

CESARE (*Going over to her, taking her hand in his*): Lady of Enduring Hope who cannot be made to set loose all that has already been taken from her, whose fingers cannot be pried open, whose mind will not trade painful hope for all the sweet release of forgetfulness, you hope that your husband will come.

JEANINE: Yes.

CESARE: That one day you will open your eyes and in some meadow filled with summer see your son reach out to touch your hand.

JEANINE: I dream that. I fall asleep on the rusted and mildewed furniture in my backyard and I dream that all this universe is nothing but the breath of a sleeping giant. That every time he breathes out a hundred billion years go by, and every time he breathes in it all collapses into nothingness again. That if only I can hold on to my son long enough some puff of breath may bring him to me again.

CESARE: Lady of Undeserved Suffering who refuses all the subtle analgesics of God, defying the will that cannot be defied, daring to remember, daring to hope, do you know what this giant dreams?

JEANINE: We are each other's dream. He dreams he is me sleeping in the sun dreaming I am him. And having gone around in a circle to which there is neither end nor answer given to anything, I open my eyes in the office of my husband's lawyers, or on the stone platform of a bus stop in Sewickley, watching the blossoms of snow fall down, weighing down my lids, closing them again, till it seems I am lost in the middle of a dark wood, hearing only the sound of the distant sleigh of the Richelieu come to bear me away.

Cesare gently touches Jeanine's face again, and then offering his hand to his cousin once more begins to exit.

Is that the best we can do, Signor Bottivicci? Chirp our legs like crickets going down the lizard's throat?

CESARE (*Turning to her*): It's a song, Mrs. Cendrars. In the mouth of annihilation, it's a stunning song.

The door in the mural swings open, and Cesare Bottivicci and his cousin disappear through it, the door closing of itself behind them. Now, with the Botticiccis gone, there is heard the low moan of wind. The open space on the back wall, accepted until now as an enormous clear glass window, suddenly expands, the walled sides of it pulling away, revealing itself for what it has always truly been—a vast empty hole. The snow that has begun to fall now blows into the room, as it does onto the terrace and the mountains beyond. Jeanine sits down in the large thronelike chair, and picking up her glass of champagne holds it in her trembling hand. The servants enter and placing themselves behind the sweet table begin putting out the candles. As each candle is extinguished, the room darkens until only Jeanine, the terrace, and the distant mountains are illuminated.

LESTER (*Glancing over the sweet table*): So much left over.
ANTHONY: Take some home for the missus.
LESTER: Still . . . so much left over.
ANTHONY (*Snuffing the last candle*): Always.

Cathy enters on the terrace, singing Johannes Brahms' "Mädchenlied," Opus 107, no. 5. Led by Dr. Atmos, the guests of the Richelieu, with the sole exception of the Bottiviccis, cross the terrace, tightening their coats against the wind and blown snow. When they are gone, it is only Cathy who remains, singing now directly to Jeanine. In the distance the sleighs of the Richelieu, bells jingling, begin to depart, and then bells and singer are lost in the rising howl of wind that seems to blow through the very halls and rooms of the Richelieu. The crystal champagne glass slips from Jeanine Cendrars' fingers and shatters on the floor. The cone of light left on her alone contracts to nothing.

END OF PLAY

THE RUG MERCHANTS OF CHAOS

For Susan Dietz and Lenny Beer,
and for
Samuel Gelfman, agent extraordinaire.

The Rug Merchants of Chaos was first presented at the Pasadena Playhouse, Pasadena, California, April 19, 1991, by Susan Dietz in association with the Pasadena Playhouse. David Schramm directed. The scenery was designed by Deborah Raymond and Dorian Vernacchio, the lighting by Kevin Mahan, the costumes by Florence Kemper and the sound by Jack Allaway. The cast was as follows:

Sheila Finkelberg ....Fran Drescher
Victor Finkelberg...Matt Landers
Annie Mottram ....Barbara Whinnery
Max Mottram...James Morrison
Captain Nakamochi ....Ernest Harada

Production was made possible, in part, by a major grant from the Fund for New American Plays, a project of the John F. Kennedy Center for the Performing Arts with support from the American Express Company in cooperation with the President's Committee on the Arts and the Humanities.

CHARACTERS

SHEILA FINKELBERG
VICTOR FINKELBERG
ANNIE MOTTRAM
MAX MOTTRAM
CAPTAIN NAKAMOCHI

TIME

Mid 1980s.

PLACE

Act One
Scene 1: The officers' lounge on the freighter *Buena Vista*. Cape Town, South Africa. Evening.
Scene 2: The lounge. The following morning.

Act Two
Scene 1: The ship's deck. That afternoon.
Scene 2: The deck. That evening.

ACT ONE

The scrim is an oriental rug, hanging in space between the audience and the set.

Kabuki music, followed by the low crackling of flames.

The rug rolls up as if consumed by the flames, revealing the fully stage-lit set behind: the officers' lounge on the freighter Buena Vista. *The* Buena Vista *is in decrepit condition, and the lounge is a microcosm of it: a couple of cheap plastic-covered couches, worn, with stuffing coming out; some easy chairs in similar condition; a fold-away card table with fold-away chairs; a beaten-up plywood bar with an old refrigerator. Upstage center a door leads out to the deck. Downstage left another door leads to a bathroom.*

The crackling of flames dies away. The kabuki music dies away.

Blackout.

Lights slowly come up again to full on the set.

Scene 1

The officers' lounge. Mid 1980's. Evening.

The Buena Vista *is in the process of completing its loading. The summer night is brutally hot and tempers are short. From somewhere off in the distance we hear the sound of a squealing winch, and someone screaming out in Spanish, "Watch what you're doing, you motherless imbecile! You're slamming the crate into the bulkhead!" The reply, equally ill-tempered, is in Japanese: "Let the whore that gave birth to you load the ship then! The gears are rusted. Nothing can be done better!" Through the upstage door that leads to the deck, four people enter, one after the other. Through the frame of the doorway, in the far distance, a fire is burning—the sky filled with a red glow, the muted sound of fire engines. Sheila Finkelberg is exhausted, and everything about her is in disarray, from the cockeyed hat on her head to the glaze in her eyes. In spite of the heat, she is wearing a large heavy-looking sealskin coat, and under it, unseen at the moment, layer upon layer of sweaters and blouses that have so puffed her out she looks like an overinflated Kewpie doll rooted to the ground in thick crepe-soled walking shoes. Sheila's arms are filled with everything hands and fingers can hold onto: one side of her body clutching a suitcase, a pair of hideously terrifying African spirit masks, a Waterford crystal lamp complete with pleated linen shade; the other side a half dozen purses dangling by their straps, a wooden fertility goddess with pendulous breasts and pregnant belly, and a fair-sized VCR, its assorted tentacular cables trailing the floor like some earthbound electronic octopus. For some moments, crushed by the weight of her enormous burden, she just stands there, and then her eyes begin slowly glancing about the room, her head scarcely turning as if afraid to see what it is she is seeing. Her eyes eventually come to rest on the back half of a rat lurking in the vicinity of the bar. Motionless, she stares at the half-exposed body of the rat, until with a twitch of its tail it vanishes. Sheila stares blankly forward again.*

SHEILA: Oh, God.

The second to enter is Annie Mottram. Annie is a tall, slender, shapely woman, as beautiful in face as she is graceful in motion. The dress she wears, though not overtly provocative, does little to conceal her figure. In one hand she holds her purse, and a nicely framed small Picasso print; in her other hand a makeup case. The third to enter is her husband, Max. What is immediately obvious about Max is that both his hands are completely bandaged, and he holds them out carefully in front. The cuffs on Max's white shirt have been rolled up in order to bandage his hands, and his tie hangs loosely around his unbuttoned collar. The last to enter is Sheila's husband, Victor. He more than any-

one else at the present moment, is the main beast of burden, lugging two suitcases with each arm, and a fully packed army duffle bag slung around his body. Part of his right trouser leg and the right side of his suit jacket are charred or burnt away. Loaded down as he is, pulled backward by the weight of the duffle bag, almost stuck in the narrow frame of the doorway, he nevertheless manages to kick the door shut before he dumps his burdens down and hastens over to his wife.

VICTOR: Here, let me help you.

SHEILA: Oh, God.

VICTOR (*Attempting to pry loose her fingers, set now as if in rigor mortis around the luggage*): You have to let go of the death masks, Sheila, so I can get the lamp out.

SHEILA: Finito. End of the line. End of the trail. Kaput. Finished. Defunct. Dodo.

VICTOR: Just take it easy, sweetheart. Everything is going to be all right.

SHEILA: The place where roaches go when they die. Ruined. Washed up. Done for. Dead.

VICTOR (*As her fingers begin opening*): You're doing just fine, sweetheart. Absolutely fine. The worst is all over with now. Isn't that right, Max?

MAX: Absolutely, Vic. Everything's under control now.

Hardly said when a distant fire engine wails.

SHEILA: Oh, God. I can smell the smoke coming from all those rugs even over here.

VICTOR: I don't think you can really do that, sweetheart. We're a long way from the warehouse.

SHEILA: Hundreds and hundreds of rugs burning.

ANNIE: She may be smelling the smoke from your suit, Victor.

VICTOR: The suit's perfectly all right. It's just a little charred, that's all.

ANNIE: Well, something's burning. I smell it, too.

VICTOR (*Smelling his suit, lifting up his leg to smell his shoes, the singed hair on his calf, ending up crazily hopping about the cabin on one leg while he sniffs*): I don't know. Maybe it's the shoe. Maybe it's the hair. I can't smell anything because of the gasoline.

SHEILA: This is all so unacceptable.

VICTOR (*Coming to rest near the door, opening it, listening to the sound of the fire engines*): I can't believe those guys are making such a big fuss out of a lousy piss-on-it and put-it-out warehouse fire.

MAX: Maybe you ought to shut the door, Vic. Keep the noise out.

VICTOR: I've seen a padful of helicopters go up with thousands of gallons of gasoline get put out faster than that. (*Shutting the door, a large flake of rust coming off in his hand*) We got ourselves on one hell of a garbage scow, Max. This ship's got rust flakes coming off it the size of Ritz crackers.

MAX: Well, let's not worry about that now. This ship's probably been around the world a thousand times, and it'll probably go around another thousand times after we're off it.

ANNIE: It's a garbage scow, Max. A garbage scow taking on God knows what to God knows where.

VICTOR: I didn't mean what I said as a complaint, Max. I know you got us on the best ship you could. It's just that if there's anything I can't stand it's people who are put in charge of a good piece of equipment and let it get oxidized into a piece of shit. They oughta take people like that out and shoot 'em!

SHEILA: I think the best thing I can do is pass out.

MAX: Look, people, I know this ship isn't exactly the *Queen Elizabeth*, but it's really not that bad. As soon as Captain Nakamochi shows us to our cabins, and we're out of the harbor, I'm sure we're all going to feel a lot better.

VICTOR: I thought he said his name was Nakamoto.

MAX: No. It's Nakamochi.

VICTOR: Is that what it sounded like to you, Annie?

SHEILA: For God's sake, who cares what his name is? Nakamoto! Nakamochi! Charlie the Tuna! Peter the Pan! I think I *am* going to pass out!

Doing almost exactly that, her legs buckling under her, swooning backwards and just caught by Victor and Annie.

ANNIE (*As the two of them pull her, heels dragging, over to the couch*): If you took off that damn coat you wouldn't feel as if you're going to pass out!

VICTOR: Come on, hon, she's right. Let me help you off with your coat.

ANNIE: It's gotta be a hundred and ten degrees in here and she's walking around with that moronic fur coat of hers on!

VICTOR: (*Tugging at the wooden statue Sheila still clutches*) Give me the statue.

SHEILA: Leave it alone!

VICTOR: I can't help you off with your coat if you won't let go of the statue.

SHEILA: Every time I get something it gets taken away!

VICTOR: You can't sit here with a fur coat on in the middle of summer, Sheila. Your face is all broken out in a sweat. You're going to end up unconscious.

SHEILA (*Still fending them off*): Why is this happening to me? I used to live in a three-story brick house in Riverdale. I had a little backyard with a swingset in it. I used to go to Bennington.

ANNIE (*Her patience exhausted*): You've got to take off your coat! It's not going to get taken away. Now, come on before I pull it off. I mean it, Sheila. If you don't let me take it off, I'm going to tear the fur and rip it off! Now stand up! Put down that stupid bloated statue and stand up!

Sheila, momentarily intimidated, does what she's told and allows the coat to be removed. Underneath is another coat, a cashmere.

For God's sake, how many coats do you have on? (*To Victor*) See if there's some ice in that fridge I can use for a compress. (*Practically tearing off Sheila's endless layers of clothing*) Coats and coats and sweaters and sweaters!

Reaching the end as Sheila modestly protects her final layer of clothing.

Now lie down. Put your feet up.

As Sheila reaches for some of the more valuable items that have been wrenched from her.

Let go of those damn things, lunatic, and lie down! Put your feet up and lie down! (*To Victor, as she picks up a girlie magazine from the floor and begins to fan the prostrate Sheila*) Is there any ice in there . . . water?

VICTOR: No. Just a yogurt with a mold on it, and some rotting fruit. (*Taking the container out, holding it up in all its blue and green and purple glory*) Christ, is that ugly!

ANNIE: All right, come over here and fan her then. Does anybody know when this boat is supposed to get under way?

MAX: Not long. Just as soon as they finish with the loading.

ANNIE: Well, they must have turned something on because I can feel the vibration coming up through my legs. It wasn't doing that before.

MAX: I think it's just the loading winch. It's probably jammed up.

SHEILA: Or maybe it's the water rats trying to get off this ship! This whole ship makes me want to throw up!

VICTOR: Hey, come on, Sheila. I know this situation isn't ideal, but let's just try and make the best of it. Okay? The only one really hurting here is Max.

SHEILA: I want to get up now.

ANNIE: I think you'd better stay down for a while.

SHEILA: I don't want to stay down. I want to sit up. I want to see what's happening here. (*Brushing the magazine in Victor's hand aside*)

ANNIE: At least let him keep fanning you.

SHEILA: I don't need giant sex organs waving in and out of focus in front of my face! (*To Victor*) And why in the name of sanity didn't you get out of that suit? Are you trying to advertise to everyone what we did? I told you to throw it in the incinerator, destroy it.

VICTOR: I didn't have time to destroy it! I was too busy following your instructions to pack an entire two-bedroom apartment into a suitcase! If you gave me another thirty seconds I probably could have jammed in the last leg of the Steinway, too!

MAX: If I can have everybody's attention for a second, I'd like to say something.

SHEILA (*Rooting through her purse*): I'd like to know where my cigarettes are. (*Pulling the last remaining cigarette out of a pack*) I'd like to know how it's possible to shove an entire pack of cigarettes into my purse and have it turn into a single cigarette!

VICTOR: Don't do that, Sheila.

SHEILA: Do what?

ANNIE: Interrupt him when he's trying to say something.

SHEILA: Well, excusez-moi. What is this? Everybody-gang-up-on-Sheila time again.

MAX: Nobody's ganging up on you, Sheila.

SHEILA: The hell you're not. Everytime I open my mouth you're all always coming down on me.

ANNIE: That's not true!

SHEILA: I can't even wonder what happened to my pack of cigarettes without there being a general attack.

VICTOR: If you've got something to say, just say it, Sheila.

SHEILA: I don't have anything I want to say . . . not in this hostile environment.

VICTOR: Go ahead, Max.

SHEILA: Nobody else here smokes so what does it matter if Sheila's down to her last cigarette? (*She contemplates whether or not to smoke her final cigarette, staring at it, rolling it around in her fingers*) Abstinence is good for Sheila. Self-denial is even better. (*Looking directly at them*) How easy it is to bear the suffering of others. (*Finally finished contemplating and complaining, she lights the cigarette*)

VICTOR: That's it? Go ahead, Max.

MAX: I just wanted to say that the four of us have been together . . . what is it? Fourteen, fifteen years now? And we've had some times when things looked like they were going to go pretty well for us, and some times when we really got the rug pulled out from under us.

SHEILA: The rug? Did anyone hear the metaphor he just used?

MAX (*Ignoring the interruption*): I guess this is just one of those times. I wish I could say that tomorrow we'd all wake up and be strolling down some nice boulevard in Buenos Aires or someplace, but the truth is tomorrow we're going to be a couple of hundred miles out in the South Atlantic, and maybe things are going to be a bit uncertain for a while.

VICTOR: We'll do okay, Max. Same as always.

MAX: Right. So . . . (*Clapping his hands inadvertently as he always does when feeling enthusiastic, and this time receiving a jolt of pain for it*) So I guess that's about all I wanted to say except that I want you all to know that we're going to come out of this all right, and that we should bear in mind that lots of people in this world have been in far worse positions than we are now and managed to make it through a hell of a lot better than they expected. Not to get too grandiose about it—and Sheila'll bear me out on this with her literature background—there were the Spartans at Thermopylae, the English at Agincourt, the Russians at Stalingrad—

SHEILA: The Spartans got wiped out at Thermopylae.

MAX (*Somewhat lost in his own thoughts*): I'm sorry. I didn't hear what you said, Sheila.

VICTOR: Go on, Max. It doesn't matter.

MAX: No. I'd really like to get Sheila's input on this.

Sheila just blows smoke rings.

VICTOR: She said the Spartans got wiped out at Thermopylae, Max.

MAX: Did they? I thought they won a victory there.

SHEILA (*Suddenly leaping to her feet, exploding in crazed triumph*): They got their ass kicked in at Thermopylae! They got wiped out to the last man at Thermopylae!

ANNIE: For God's sake, what difference does it make? That's not what he's talking about!

SHEILA (*Pounding her feet in a frantic jig*): I went to Bennington and I know what happened to the Spartans at Thermopylae!

VICTOR: Who gives a shit what happened a million years ago, Sheila!

SHEILA: It's like everything he says! It sounds right, but when you know what he's talking about, it's not right!

VICTOR: Go on, Max. Finish up what you wanted to say.

MAX: No, that's about it. I . . . um . . . ah . . . (*Running on for a few seconds as if there might be something further he wants to say, and then stopping*) That's it.

VICTOR: I think I saw a bottle behind the bar. Does anyone want a drink?

Annie shakes her head. Max and Sheila give no sign one way or the other. Victor heads over towards the bar.

SHEILA: I'd like to know what we're going to do if the police get here before this boat leaves the harbor.

VICTOR: They're not going to get here. They probably won't even begin to sort this thing out till tomorrow.

SHEILA: Is that right, Max? Because you know how much we've all come to rely on your judgment. Or maybe you'd like to tell us again how swell it's all going to be once our warehouse is nothing but a three-alarm fire and we're all sitting around collecting our insurance checks?

VICTOR: Damn it, Sheila! Will you get off his back?

MAX: We were drowning in excess inventory. I don't know what else we could have done.

SHEILA: A hundred and eight genuine Bukharas made in Allentown, Pennsylvania; sixty-seven Peking Orientals made in Hoboken, New Jersey; two hundred and ninety-two native Indian Dhurries handcrafted in an Albanian shirt factory. That's some excess-inventory problem, Max.

ANNIE: You want to get into all of that, Sheila, I'd like to hear something about your husband's special Shahistan purchase!

MAX: Annie, please . . .

ANNIE: Two hundred and eighteen hand-knotted Iranians in butterfly design that lost their wings and antenna with the first good foot-wipe!

VICTOR: I did my best on that, Annie.

MAX: She knows you did, Vic. Come on, Annie, let's not—

VICTOR: I spoke to buyers from Durban, Alexandria, Luanda. They were all buying them.

ANNIE: I bet they were.

VICTOR: They were! And we got the best price of all!

ANNIE: Of course we did! You bought ten times as many as anyone else!

VICTOR: That's not true. The buyer from Luanda bought almost four hundred Iranians at three dollars more per rug.

MAX: He's right, Annie. That's the truth.

VICTOR: Then why is she ragging me about that now? You go out in the market and you buy enough rugs, sooner or later you're going to come up with a bad batch. Who the hell ever said I was supposed to be infallible?

ANNIE: Not me.

MAX: Will you stop it, Annie? Just stop it!

VICTOR: If I was infallible I'd be sitting in the Vatican with a yarmulke on my head!

ANNIE: That's right! People who are infallible don't spill gasoline all over themselves! Don't knock over lighted candles so my husband has to burn his hands beating the flames off them! If it wasn't for you, we'd be sitting around the dinner table right now, waiting for the fire department to call, carving up Sheila's chic-chic duck flambeau with couscous and peanut sauce!

The door opens and Captain Nakamochi enters, just in time to catch the final moments of the argument. The Captain is a short grungy-looking man, dressed in a soiled undershirt and a worn captain's hat. His teeth are bad, his body and arms tattooed.

CAPTAIN (*Flashing his usual smile, as he looks them over*): Good evening. I am Captain Nakamochi. Welcome aboard my ship. You are all comfortable?

MAX: Yes. We are. Thank you, Captain. I'm sorry I didn't have the chance to introduce my wife and friends to you when we came on board, but you seemed rather busy with the loading.

CAPTAIN: Loading all finished now.

MAX: Good. Captain, I'd like you to meet my wife, Annie, and this is Mr. and Mrs. Finkelberg.

VICTOR: How do you do?

CAPTAIN (*To Max, after staring up and down Annie*): Your wife very tall.

MAX: Yes, she is.

CAPTAIN (*Flashing another one of his usual smiles, which hardly ever seems to be connected to the immediate situation*): I want you all to be comfortable. You want something all you do is ask.

MAX: That's very generous of you, Captain Nakamochi. We appreciate that.

CAPTAIN: Food, drink . . . whatever you need. (*Positioning himself for the moment directly in front of Annie*) The *Buena Vista* is a very comfortable ship . . . (*Slapping his stomach to show her how hard it is*) . . . excellent condition. (*Jiggling his hand in his pocket as if his penis were jumping about*) It has everything you need. You are all Americans?

MAX: Yes.

SHEILA (*Simultaneously, her voice tinged with the cynicism of one who expects to be swindled*): Yeah. You bet we are.

CAPTAIN: I like Americans. Americans very generous people.

MAX: Thank you.

CAPTAIN: Land of the free. Home of the brave. Junk bonds. Easy come, easy go.

The captain laughs. Max tries to join in, not too successfully.

ANNIE: Captain? Could we be shown to our cabins?

CAPTAIN: Cabins?

ANNIE: Yes. Where we sleep.

CAPTAIN: Ah, I understand. Your cabins. Where you sleep.

ANNIE: Yes.

CAPTAIN: This is your cabins.

SHEILA: Oh, God! Here it comes.

ANNIE: But this is a lounge. I'm talking about where we sleep. Our rooms.

CAPTAIN: Yes, this is where you sleep. Very comfortable.

ANNIE: But there are four of us. Don't you have two cabins? Two separate rooms? Private.

CAPTAIN: This is private. Nobody comes here. You see, here are your couches, chairs, table—

SHEILA: Oh, God.

CAPTAIN (*Opening up the bathroom door to reveal a visible hellhole*): Nice toilet with shower and washbasin. (*Going over to the refrigerator*) Nice refrigerator for your food. (*Opening it to reveal another hellhole*) Ah, you see, somebody has already put food in.

ANNIE (*In desperation*): Max?

MAX: Captain Nakamochi? (*Walking aside with him*) I don't think this is going to work out. What we need are two separate cabins, with beds or bunks in them. I indicated that to you when I first spoke to you three days ago, remember?

CAPTAIN: You said you wanted perhaps passage on my ship. Even that was not certain. It was perhaps.

MAX: Well, it's definite now. You do have cabins on this ship, don't you?

CAPTAIN: Oh yes, very nice cabins.

MAX: Good.

CAPTAIN: Three cabins.

MAX: Well, that's fine.

Victor, Annie, and Sheila in anticipation of the move begin picking up their belongings.

What we'd like are two of them.

CAPTAIN: One cabin for me and woman. One cabin for first officer and woman. Third cabin for crew—eighteen men and no woman.

As the captain's words sink in, the luggage begins dropping back to the floor.

You will be comfortable here, okay, for sure. (*Walking over to the bar*) You bring whiskey for yourself?

MAX: No.

CAPTAIN: I get you whiskey, scotch, piña colada . . . whatever you like. (*Picking up the whiskey bottle*) This bottle only fifty dollars.

VICTOR: That bottle is half empty.

CAPTAIN: Full bottle one hundred dollars. You bring food for yourself?

VICTOR: No. Who brings his own food on board a ship?

CAPTAIN: Okay, for sure. I have food sent in for you: octopus, squid, sea urchin, fresh pineapple juice. You don't like pineapple juice, I have grapefruit juice, whole oranges. All American favorites. Breakfast twenty dollars with cook's special eggs in seaweed. Twenty-five dollars without cook's special eggs in seaweed. (*Laughing at his own joke*)

SHEILA: Oh, God.

CAPTAIN: Lunch thirty dollars. Dinner fifty dollars. Fresh coffee extra. Cheesecake double extra.

MAX: I thought everything was supposed to be included in our passage. You take a cruise somewhere you don't pay extra for your food.

CAPTAIN: Everything, how you say, à la carte. You give me your passage money now, please.

MAX: Half now, half when we get there. Right?

CAPTAIN: Okay, for sure.

MAX: Give him the money, Annie.

Annie opens her purse and taking out an envelope, hands it to Captain Nakamochi.

CAPTAIN (*Counting the money*): Only two thousand dollars here.

VICTOR: That's right! Five hundred each now, another five hundred each when we get there! Four thousand dollars in all! That's what you agreed on with him, wasn't it?

CAPTAIN: No! No! One thousand each now. One thousand each again when you get off.

VICTOR: Eight thousand dollars! You want eight thousand dollars! (*He takes a step toward the captain*)

MAX (*More or less blocking Victor*): Take it easy, Vic.

VICTOR: What the hell is happening here, Max? I thought you had an agreement with him.

MAX: I did! Let's all calm down, shall we? Captain Nakamochi is a reasonable man. I'm sure we can work this out to everybody's satisfaction.

CAPTAIN: Okay, for sure. Four thousand dollars now, four thousand dollars in Tasmania.

SHEILA: Tasmania? This boat is going to Tasmania?

MAX: Can we get into that a little later, Sheila?

SHEILA: Where the fuck is Tasmania?

MAX: Not now, Sheila! Captain Nakamochi has to get his *ship out of the harbor as quickly as possible*! (*Turning his attention back to the captain*) If we pay what you're asking we're not going to have any money left when we arrive in Tasmania. We're going to be stranded.

CAPTAIN: Okay, for sure.

MAX: No. Not okay for sure. Now suppose we stick to our original agreement, plus I will throw in an additional personal bonus for you of five hundred dollars. That's forty-five hundred dollars in all.

CAPTAIN: You pay me seven thousand dollars and I throw in personal bonus *for you*—breakfast for free. Not à la carte.

MAX: Five thousand, and with all the meals.

CAPTAIN: No other ships in harbor.

MAX: That's my final offer, Captain. It's quite fair.

CAPTAIN: Big fire out there. Sparks fall all over Cape Town. (*When*

Max doesn't respond) You do something to your hands?

VICTOR: Yeah. He had an industrial accident.

CAPTAIN (*Looking at the two men for a moment and then breaking out in a laugh*): That very funny. I like that. Industrial accident. (*Suddenly stopping his laugh*) Okay. Five thousand. Food à la carte.

MAX: Included.

CAPTAIN: Food much better when it is à la carte.

MAX: We'll be happy to eat whatever you eat, Captain.

For a long moment the captain just stands there studying his adversary, and then, obviously deciding that he's wrung out everything he's going to, breaks out into another one of his false unpredictable laughs. First Max, then Victor, then Annie force themselves to join in. Sheila, alone, doesn't bother.

SHEILA: Oh, pul . . . eeze!

CAPTAIN (*Abruptly all business*): Rest of down payment.

MAX: Give him the other five hundred dollars, Annie.

Annie takes out another envelope from her purse, placing the hundred-dollar bills one by one in Captain Nakamochi's outstretched hand. When he walks away, opening the door to the deck, the sky seems redder than before, the sound of sirens louder.

CAPTAIN: Hot time in the old town tonight.

Offering up another one of his unpredictable laughs, he exits, leaving the door open behind him. Max hastens over and shuts it, leaning his back against it, lost in his own thoughts, as Victor heads over to the bar).

VICTOR: That guy reminds me of the six-inch millipede that crawled up my leg one night at Vinh Long, or Da Linh, or Phan Rang. I'm down on the ground trying to get some sleep because I haven't slept for about two months and I feel like shit and I look like shit, when I feel this thing coming up the inside of my pants leg like a wave. I don't know what the hell it is. I'm so fucking tired I don't even know if I'm dreaming it. (*Pours out his drink*) Meanwhile, it's rippling through my pubic hair, undulating up my groin, and I'm scared shit to move and I'm scared shit to bang down on it because I don't think I can kill anything that size in one shot, and God knows how many fangs the fucking thing's probably got. Pretty soon it's up outta my chest and palpating my lips with its front two hundred and fifty feet. I want to scream out and fling this thing away from me, when it rears up and looks me right in the eye. And that was when I saw it. The thing had a face! And I could tell from the way it was swiveling it around it was as lost as I was. It had black eyes and a little yellow face . . . and it was as lost as I was! (*Swallowing his drink*)

SHEILA: What am I doing here? Why am I on a boat that's going to Tasmania? My parents saved up all their life to give me a first-class education with the WASPs at Bennington. I slept in a room with a girl named Muffin who had six pairs of opera gloves, a face like diaper rash, and ended up marrying Standard Oil of New Jersey!

VICTOR: It's all going to work out, Sheila. Stop driving yourself wacko.

SHEILA: Literature majors of the Italian Renaissance are not arsonists by nature! (*Directly at Victor*) Chemistry majors from Cornell are not arsonists by nature!

ANNIE: Nobody's an arsonist by nature, Sheila.

VICTOR (*To Sheila*): Will you take it easy?

SHEILA: Why? (*Pointing toward Max*) Because that's what he always says? "Take it easy. Take it easy" while he moves us all along like cows down the executioner's chute! He's not going to stop until we all end up with a three-inch bolt of steel in our head! That's the way they kill cows, you know. I read all about it in a book exposing the meat-packing industry!

VICTOR: We've had a lousy day, Sheila, that's all. You'll feel better in the morning when you've had a good night's sleep.

SHEILA: Nothing works out! The Big Brain's resort business in Tampico didn't work out! Fix it up! Sell it to Club Med! It's got a climate just like Cuba's!

VICTOR: The deal almost went through, you know that. If that hurricane didn't come up and blow half our beach cabanas into the Gulf of Mexico—

SHEILA: "If" doesn't do anything! "Almost" is failure! The neon-light business that didn't work out in Panama City! The synthetic perfume he had you brewing up that smelled just like Chanel No. 5 for two dollars an ounce that didn't work out in Montevideo!

ANNIE: It worked out good enough for you to buy a fur coat out of it!

VICTOR: That perfume was every bit as good as Chanel No. 5. There was enough profit margin there to set us up for life if women were smart enough to purchase quality instead of labels.

SHEILA: Right! And that's the excuse for the soda syrup that was supposed to taste better than Coca-Cola, only it stuck to your teeth like epoxy and had to have a city permit just to be poured down the sewer?

MAX (*Suddenly, calmly, entering the conversation*): When you're undercapitalized and forced to brew syrup formulas using milk bottles for test tubes, Sheila, these things occur. However, the truth of the matter is that any one of our business ventures could have just as easily caught fire as failed and made the four of us extremely wealthy.

SHEILA: "Caught fire"? Did anybody notice the metaphor he just used?

MAX: I think you realize as well as any of us that every business venture has a certain element of risk attached to it that must be balanced against the opportunity for decent capital appreciation. The phone didn't work on day one for Alexander Graham Bell. The radium didn't come out of the pitchblende on day one for Madame Curie.

SHEILA: The Dreyfus Lion speaks. The man of many disguises and situations: mining engineer and real estate developer, perfume manufacturer and salesman of the unsellable Mont Blanc Cola—the only cola in the world to have an injunction slapped against it by a pen company! (*Holding her hands out, raising them up and down, salaaming*) Whereto now, O Wise One?

MAX: Wherever it is at least it's not going to be without our initial seed supply.

SHEILA: And what does that mean?

MAX: It means, dear Sheila, that though we may never have seen these particular seeds ripen into fruit, yet they remain intact.

SHEILA: Does anybody know what he's talking about, because I don't. We don't have any seed supply, Max. You gave it all away to Captain Nakamochi.

MAX: Not quite. It's true we would have had even more if Captain Nakamochi hadn't unjustly seized a business opportunity and upped the ante, but what we have is not insufficient for our purposes.

VICTOR: We've got three thousand dollars more, Sheila.

ANNIE: It's under the bandages. When I wrapped his hands he gave it to me to put under his bandages.

SHEILA: How can we have three thousand dollars more? After we paid off Nakamochi we were supposed to be down to nothing!

VICTOR: Max pulled it out of the business the first six months, while we were still making a profit.

MAX: You see, Sheila, the average individual when faced with a difficult or seemingly insoluble problem tends to think of solutions in terms of either-or. Either I go left or right, buy or sell, up or down—

SHEILA (*To Victor*): How long did you know about this?

VICTOR: Just this evening.

MAX (*Continuing without pause through Sheila's interruption*): . . . The truth of the matter is that there is always at least another alternative, and most probably an infinite number of them. Faced with the choice of either distributing our initial profits or using them to expand our inventory in hopes of enlarging the business, I simply chose the unexpected alternative—I buried it in the cat's litter box at the warehouse.

SHEILA: You kept thousands of dollars buried in that stinking urinous litter box all these years without telling anyone?

MAX: I didn't see any reason to divulge this particular information. If the business had succeeded, the money would have been freed up. If things went the other way, our basic seed supply was secure.

SHEILA: And who gave you the right to make that decision without consulting anybody?

VICTOR: It was the right decision, Sheila. If he hadn't put the money aside, it just would have gone down the tubes like the rest of it. We'd have nothing. At least now we can begin again.

SHEILA: And what would have happened if that goddamn cat's urine had soaked down to the bills and eaten them up? God knows it stunk bad enough all these years.

MAX: Oh, there wasn't any cat. There was just the litter box. I sprinkled ammonia into it every day to smell like cat urine. I always thought one of you would have asked me why the litter box was always wet when nobody ever saw a cat, but nobody did. (*Offering up a little laugh, which when nobody joins in he quickly suppresses, changing the topic*) I'd better see Nakamochi about getting some bedding in here.

VICTOR: Get a fan, too, Max. The air is suffocating in here.

Max nods his head as he exits. Sheila heads for the bathroom.

Where you going?

SHEILA: To the bathroom. I haven't had a chance to piss in eight hours.

VICTOR: You'd better put some toilet paper down on that seat. I wouldn't just sit on it.

SHEILA: I don't need directions from you on how to protect my ass!

(*Closing the bathroom door behind her*)

ANNIE: It bothers you he didn't tell you about the money, doesn't it?

VICTOR: Hey . . . listen . . . if I had wanted to know about it, I would have asked . . . right? It's okay. This way I just follow instructions. It's better that way for me.

SHEILA: Oh, God! There are things moving in here!

ANNIE: We'll get some cleanser tomorrow and clean this whole place up.

SHEILA: I can't stand living in filth! I hate it! I hate it! (*Sound of ferocious banging, hands slapping against the bathroom walls*)

VICTOR: What are you doing in there?

SHEILA: What do you think I'm doing in here, Victor? I'm fighting for my life!

For some long moments Victor considers his wife's remarks, not sure if he's supposed to take them seriously or not; and then, when the sounds of the battle within fail to subside, concern wins out over seeming ridiculous in front of Annie, and he hastens over to the bathroom and enters. The sounds of battle are redoubled, Sheila eventually backing out of the bathroom, leaving Victor to finish the struggle.

I hate things with six legs and seven legs and eight legs . . . eyes that stick out like little balls of jelly bouncing on the end of stalks . . . feet that walk upside down on ceilings and never fall off! I hate them!

VICTOR (*Coming out of the bathroom*): It's all right. I've killed everything. You can go back in. (*When Sheila doesn't move*) Go ahead. Nothing's going to bother you in there. I wiped them all out. Everything's dead.

SHEILA: I don't have to go.

VICTOR: Of course you have to. You just said you didn't take a leak in eight hours.

SHEILA (*More pressed by her fears than by her bladder*): I exaggerated. It was only six hours.

VICTOR: Nobody exaggerates about having to go, Sheila. (*Taking her arm, escorting his unwilling wife back to the door of the bathroom*) Now stop making such a fuss while everybody else is trying to make the best of it.

SHEILA: (*Wriggling out of his grasp*): I don't have to go. I've changed my mind. It was premature. (*Sitting down on the couch, crossing her legs first one way then the other, obviously uncomfortable, obvi-*

ously trying to find some way to be comfortable)

VICTOR: It's eighteen days to Tasmania. (*Continuing to look at his wife's gymnastics*) You're going to have to start trying to make the best of things.

SHEILA: I am. I'm just sitting here, crossing my legs.

VICTOR: No, you're not, sweetheart. You're finding eggshells to pick out of your teeth, while everybody else is trying to find the eggs. You want to get off this boat? I'll get off right now with you. I swear I will.

SHEILA: And go where?

VICTOR: That's right. And go where? Because we're doing the only thing that makes sense for us to do. You wanna backtrack from there? You want to blame Max because he had enough foresight to make sure there was a way out even before the fire was set?

SHEILA: I don't want to discuss this now.

ANNIE: I think I'll go out on deck.

VICTOR: No. I want you to stay. The four of us are all a part of everything that's happening here. We're not eight legs walking in eight different directions. (*To Sheila*) You wanna backtrack from there?

SHEILA: I don't want to backtrack, Victor. I just want to sit here and think with whatever shambles are left of my mind.

VICTOR: You think there was something wrong in the way the fire was set? That was my fault. I was the one who fucked up a perfectly good plan. She's right.

Annie positively winces as her accusation is recalled.

If it hadn't of been for me, it would've worked out.

Sheila is too uncomfortable to sit any longer. She stands up, wanders about, circling and moving away from the bathroom as Victor continues his unrelenting analysis.

You wanna backtrack from there?

SHEILA: I don't wanna backtrack.

VICTOR: Once we realized the business was going under, what other options did we have besides trying to collect on the insurance? Go broke? Go into bankruptcy? Pay our creditors off a few cents on the dollar until there was nothing left of anything and what they got wouldn't have meant a hill of beans to them? You wanna backtrack from there?

SHEILA: I don't want to backtrack, Victor! I don't want to backtrack!

Suddenly there is a loud bang. The engine has kicked in, but somehow terribly wrong. It vibrates everything, including the occupants of the lounge, who shake like hapless marionettes.

ANNIE: My God, what is that?

VICTOR: I don't know.

SHEILA: The whole ship is vibrating!

ANNIE: Maybe it's the winch! Maybe the winch got jammed!

VICTOR: It can't be the winch! They stopped loading!

SHEILA: I can't vibrate like this!

VICTOR: It'll probably stop in a second! They're probably just blowing out the bilge water!

SHEILA: How can it be the bilge water? We haven't even left the harbor yet to get any bilge!

VICTOR: Then maybe it's the fuel line! How the hell do I know what it is?

SHEILA: Oh, God! Oh, God!

The sound and vibration suddenly stop. The silence is almost eerie. Nobody moves.

VICTOR (*Cautiously, after a moment*): That's it. It stopped.

For some seconds more there is silence, and they slowly release their breath.

It's over. It's finished.

The words are no sooner out of his mouth when the noise and vibration begin again. Annie, holding on to some of the furniture, finds her feet being pulled out from under her until she is stretched out face down on the floor.

SHEILA: I can't stand it! I'm losing my mind! I can't vibrate like this from here to Tasmania!

Blackout.

Kabuki music, a second time.

Lights up to a semidarkness suggestive of pale moonlight. Through the open doorway to the lounge we can see Captain Nakamochi standing on the deck, arms folded across his chest, overseeing the work of two crewmen bringing in cots and bedding. When their labors are complete, Max, Annie, Victor and Sheila are asleep. Lights fade to black. Kabuki music ends.

Scene 2

The lounge. The following morning.

The sound of what might be sumo wrestlers, grunting and groaning as their bodies collide, the sound intermittently punctuated by indecipherable shrieks and outcries. As the lights come up—shafts of morning light through the portholes, a naked bulb burning in the bathroom—we see the sleeping forms of Max, Victor and Sheila strewn about the room: Max on a cot with his hands on top of the covers; Victor on the floor with the covers thrown over his head; Sheila scrunched up on a couch. Through the open bathroom door, we can see Annie on her hands and knees scrubbing the floor. As the sound of the "sumo wrestlers" reaches a crescendo with a final bellow fading away in satisfaction, Sheila, suddenly awakened, sits bolt upright. She glances about the room, listening to the dying sound that surrounds her, and then, frightened out of her wits, slides against the wall toward Annie and the light. She taps Annie on the back and both women jump and shriek, each startled by the other.

SHEILA: Did you hear that? That ape thing.

ANNIE: It's Nakamochi through the ventilation shaft. He returned to his woman about four o'clock this morning.

SHEILA: It sounded like animals. That man is truly disgusting. I can't imagine any woman of her own free will sleeping with him. (*Watching Annie work for a second*) What are you doing?

ANNIE: I'm trying to get this place cleaned up before the filth in here drives us all whacko. I don't think this bathroom has been cleaned since this ship was launched. (*Whacking her rag at some roaches*) Out! Out!

SHEILA: How long have you been in there?

ANNIE: Since Nakamochi woke me up at four o'clock.

SHEILA: Couldn't this wait until after breakfast? You must be exhausted.

ANNIE: No. I want to get this place cleaned up before anyone has to use it again.

SHEILA: Where did you get the soap? I didn't see any soap in there last night.

ANNIE: It's not soap. It's Max's Selsun Blue. I saw all this rust in here and it seemed to me the rust was to the ship what dandruff was to the head, so I used it. (*Handing Sheila a strip of flypaper with flies all over it*) You want to get rid of this? This is very gross.

Sheila gingerly transports the flypaper over to a small plastic garbage can, but when she tries to shake it in, it sticks to her fingers. And the more she shakes the more it sticks.

I think all these flies must be the descendants of the original flies that came on this ship when it was built. Thousands and thousands of generations of flies reproducing on this ship. It really makes you wonder, doesn't it?

SHEILA: About what?

ANNIE (*Noticing that Sheila is stuck, and heading over*): About how everything manages to reproduce and go on no matter what the situation is. Rust. Whatever. (*Freeing Sheila of the flypaper, holding it in her hands and staring at it*) Even on the flypaper with their legs sticking together. Some of the flies are very tiny. Maybe they were born on the flypaper. (*Dropping the flypaper into the can*)

SHEILA: Flies don't get born as flies. They get born as maggots. Disgusting little white worms.

MAX (*Waking up*): Annie?

ANNIE (*Going over to her husband, bending down and kissing him*): Good morning, sweetheart. How do you feel?

MAX: I feel fine.

ANNIE (*Touching his forehead*): You feel a little warm.

SHEILA: Maybe it's because it's suffocating in here. It was suffocating in here last night when we didn't have the fan, and now it's suffocating in here when we do have the fan! How is it possible that nothing is improved by the improvement? Here, I will show you something. (*Striding, stumbling over the mess of bedding and belongings to the door—flinging it open*) You open the door . . . (*Standing there as if ushering in some unseen presence*) . . . it's suffocating. (*Closing the door*) You close the door . . . it's suffocating. Somewhere on this ship there is a breeze blowing. There is no object in the universe this big that does not have a breeze blowing on it somewhere!

Victor wakes up suddenly from a nightmare. His face is broken out in a sweat. He involuntarily wipes the back of his hand and his fingers across his lips, hard, and then aware of where he is, stops.

VICTOR: What time is it?

SHEILA: It's early. It's five-thirty. You had a bad night.

MAX (*Sticking his feet halfway into an old pair of sneakers, and staggering tiredly about the room*): I'll go see about our meals.

SHEILA: You also better see about getting some fresh water in here before we start shriveling up like those phony human heads you wanted to invest in in Ecuador.

Max obligingly staggers over toward the bathroom to see about the water.

VICTOR: What about the shower? Isn't there fresh water in that?

ANNIE: No. I tried it. It's salt water and it's rusty.

As Max makes a U-turn and starts back toward the door to the deck.

VICTOR: I'd like to check out Nakamochi's cabin. I'm sure that son of a bitch isn't bathing in cold salt water.

SHEILA: And tell him we want clean sheets. The sheets he gave you last night weren't very clean.

VICTOR: They looked all right to me.

SHEILA: They're not all right when there's someone else's little body hairs all over them with flakes of dead skin.

VICTOR: So you brush it off.

SHEILA: Oh, pul . . . eeze!

MAX: Look, people, I know we're all uncomfortable and hungry and grungy and everything else, so maybe if someone's got a pencil and paper we can make a list of everything we need and give it to Captain Nakamochi at one time.

VICTOR: I'll do it. I think I saw some paper and a pencil behind the bar.

MAX: If we're going to make it through the next four weeks, we're going to have to get a hell of a lot better organized than we've been so far.

SHEILA: I thought it was eighteen days. Didn't he tell us when we were coming up the gangplank it was going to be eighteen days?

VICTOR: So now it's twenty-eight days. What's the difference?

SHEILA: They've got cargo to deliver. They don't just take an extra ten days because they feel like it.

VICTOR: Let's just get on with the list, Max. I'll write it down on this bar napkin.

MAX: No. She's right. I was going to tell you this morning anyway. I just didn't want to bother you with it last night. We're going to have an extra stop in Tamatave.

SHEILA: Where the hell is Tamatave? We've lived in South Africa for four years, and I've never heard of Tamatave!

MAX: It's on the east coast of Madagascar. It's right along his route.

VICTOR: Do you know what the stop's for, Max?

MAX: Captain Nakamochi wants to get the vibration in the ship taken care of. You must have felt it last night after I left.

VICTOR: Yeah, we thought it was the bilge pump or something like that.

SHEILA: You mean you thought it was the bilge pump or something like that.

MAX: Well, anyway, he's going to take care of it in Tamatave, and then we'll be on our way again. Actually, this stopover has a lot to offer in terms of sightseeing and educational potential. Not too many people realize the enormous amount of vanilla beans that are grown on Madagascar, and that some of the best plantations available for public tours are within fifty miles of our destination in Tamatave. So we need not have to worry about being bored. (*Clapping his hands enthusiastically and wincing for it*) Okay? So let's get on with the list.

SHEILA: What was vibrating?

VICTOR: The man already told you what the problem was, Sheila.

ANNIE: The ship was vibrating.

SHEILA: That doesn't mean anything. It's like asking someone why he's going deaf and he tells you it's because he don't hear so good anymore! What's the matter with the two of you? By now we must be two hundred miles out on the ocean! Don't you want to know what's wrong with this ship?

ANNIE (*With great purposefulness*): We do know, Sheila. It's the vibration, and it'll be taken care of.

SHEILA (*Giving up on her husband and Annie*): I want to know what it is that's vibrating on this ship, Max.

MAX (*After a moment's hesitation*): The propeller shaft and the drive linkage leading to it.

SHEILA: Oh, God.

MAX: It's really not that serious.

SHEILA: Bingo. Bango. Bango. Bongo!

MAX: It's just a little mechanical problem that's going to be taken care of as soon as we reach Tamatave.

VICTOR: Okay, you happy? Now you know the truth.

SHEILA (*To Victor*): There are no little mechanical problems that take ten days! (*To Max*) If it's such a little mechanical problem, why didn't they just fix it in Cape Town before we left?

MAX: They could have fixed it in Cape Town, but I don't think we had the option of remaining there for ten more days, do you?

SHEILA: Since when does Captain Nakamochi care about our options?

MAX: Since I promised him an additional thousand dollars.

SHEILA: Hello? Does anybody here realize what he's done? He bribed that stupid greedy man with bad teeth and tattoos to sail out into the open sea with a broken-down propeller that could probably fall off at any minute and leave us stranded out here!

VICTOR: And what would you have done, Sheila? Wait for the repairs to get done in the harbor until the police came by and picked us up?

ANNIE: That's not possible, what she says, is it, Max?

MAX: Of course not. All ships have worn parts that eventually break down. Something goes, they simply make temporary repairs until they reach another port. But nothing is going to happen to this ship.

ANNIE (*To Sheila*): Why must you always make such a fuss!

SHEILA (*Ignoring Annie*): How do you know that? Do you get vibrations out of the sky that nobody else is aware of? How do you *know* that damn propeller isn't going to fall off and just leave us drifting out here?

VICTOR: For Christ sake, you think anyone could persuade a ship's captain to head out into the ocean for a thousand bucks if he didn't think his propeller was going to stay on?

SHEILA: Yes! Yes! He can persuade anybody to do anything! That's his greatest gift in life! Mr. Cocksure and Absolute Certainty!

MAX (*As calmly reassuring as ever*): Believe me, Sheila, I could not have persuaded Captain Nakamochi to take this ship out of the harbor for ten times what I gave him if he didn't think it was perfectly safe.

SHEILA: Sure you could. You persuaded my husband to give up a good research job he had waiting for him with a major pharmaceutical house so you could drag him around the globe.

VICTOR: Nobody dragged me anywhere, Sheila.

SHEILA: Tampico to Panama City, Panama City to Montevideo, Montevideo to on and on! I don't think we're ever going to stop! We're going to go on and on until we fall off the end of the earth, or die someplace nobody's ever heard of! You're right, Max. We don't have to worry about being shipwrecked at sea. We've already been shipwrecked on land, up and down two continents!

A long moment of silence.

MAX: I'll see about getting us some breakfast, and then I'll straighten out the problem with the water.

ANNIE: I'll go with you.

MAX (*Pausing at the door*): It's going to be all right. I promise you. I've been giving a lot of thought to what we're going to do once we're clear of all this, and it's all beginning to jell in my mind. I just need a little more time to put it all together. (*Exits*)

ANNIE: My husband never did anything he didn't think was the best for all of us. He's always thinking about everyone else. (*Exits after Max*)

VICTOR (*After a moment, going over to his duffle bag*): I'm going to change clothes.

SHEILA: I meant to pack away another suit for you, and I forgot.

VICTOR: It doesn't matter.

SHEILA: I can imagine what we're going to look like when this boat docks and we have to check into a hotel. She's going to come down the gangplank looking like the evening gown competition at Atlantic City and the rest of us are going to come trailing behind looking like a retinue of sewer rats.

VICTOR: There was a time you weren't so concerned about the way you looked. You used to walk around in a pair of ratty jeans with antinuke patches sewn on both haunches. You didn't shampoo your hair for six months at a time.

SHEILA: That was another world.

VICTOR: I guess it was. Your mother used to pass out every time you descended from Bennington. I used to think the only reason she approved of our engagement was that I was the only guy you knew who clipped his hair, wore a suit, and didn't have six-inch grimy toenails growing into the ground.

SHEILA: My mother adored you from the time you were five years old.

VICTOR: Is that true, really?

SHEILA: Oh, yes. The first time she saw you playing in the sandbox at Van Cortlandt Park with those big Tonka trucks you had, grinding everybody else's toys into the ground, she knew you were the right one for me. She kept pushing me to go over and play with you. "Go play with him. Go play with him."

VICTOR: I remember having a magnet—a big red one with silver tips.

SHEILA: No. It was a Tonka truck and you ran it all over my face. My mother was so certain you were going to turn out to be a corporate executive. She should only have known that fifteen years later you'd be the only one in all our crowd who took his ROTC commission seriously and signed up for that . . . place.

VICTOR: Your mother really wanted a corporate executive for you, she should've backed one of your friends with the six-inch grimy toenails and the guitar slung over his back. None of them had any trouble when the time was right switching over to the *Wall Street Journal* and the Countess Mara tie. There must have been some run on the barber shops the morning the great conversion took place. I wish I could have been there to see it: ten trillion tons of hair clumping to the floor, ten trillion guitar strings snapping right in the middle of "Blowing in the Wind." I used to wonder where all those pawn shops got all those guitars. Now we know, don't we?

SHEILA (*Abruptly changing the topic*): What are we going to do when we get off this boat?

VICTOR: You know what my favorite moment was in that whole goddamn war? Coming back to perfect California: the perfect band playing, the perfect brass all lined up giving perfect hand salutes on the perfect tarmac—and you, prettier than I had ever remembered you, holding onto your perfect straw hat, the wind blowing your skirt. Everything perfect, except as we drive out the gate, some woman holding a placard over her head smashes it down against the windshield, calling me a murderer and a savage. As if she knew one fucking thing of what anything was about!

SHEILA: Do you know what we're going to do when this boat docks?

VICTOR: We'll figure out something.

SHEILA: We haven't figured out anything since we ran into them at that taco stand in L.A. He's going off the deep end, and she's not far behind. You should have heard her in the bathroom this morning, going after the rust with the Selsun Blue because the rust was like dandruff.

VICTOR: What difference does it make what she used, if she did the job?

SHEILA (*Slightly imitating Annie*): I think these flies must be the descendants of the original flies that came on this ship when it was built . . . thousands and thousands of hairy flies reproducing on this ship. (*Dropping the attempt at imitation*) And when I asked her what the hell she was talking about, she tells me in that euphonious little voice of hers how the flies are reproducing on the flypaper, giving birth to little flies while their little legs are all stuck together.

VICTOR: There's nothing wrong with her, and there's nothing wrong with him.

SHEILA: Of course. That explains why, when he isn't burying money in the cat's litter box and pouring ammonia on it to make it smell like urine, he sounds like the Dreyfus Lion addressing a colloquium at the Harvard Business School.

VICTOR: You're just pissed off because the fire in the warehouse didn't work out the way we wanted it to.

SHEILA: Not the way "we" wanted it to. The way Max wanted it. He was the one who thought of it. He was the one who pushed for it.

VICTOR: So what? There's always someone who gets the idea first. What are you doing, Sheila? Practicing what you're going to say to the prosecution? You put someone in charge, you show him loyalty. You stick with him.

SHEILA: I never put him in charge. I never approved of setting that fire. The very first time it was mentioned to me I called it an immoral unethical act.

VICTOR: Well, that really put the skids to it, didn't it? About as much as those letters you used to write me, telling me, in the middle of pulling shit-smeared punji sticks out of the feet of my men, I was engaged in an immoral war. I used to try envisioning you scribbling away on those letters in the Bennington library—

SHEILA: Don't! Don't you do that to me . . . take letters I wrote out of love and reduce them to political statements! I didn't only sit up in the library writing letters to you! I sat up in my bed in the middle of the night, holding my chest, feeling my body shaking, going through month after month of agony because I felt you were never coming home again. That you were going to go on and on with that war until you got yourself killed! You know what kind of wound that put in me? I wanted so much to be with you when I heard you were coming home, I took the first plane I could get to California. I wanted to be the first face you saw when you came down those steps. You think we got married in Los Angeles on the spur of the moment, just like that? Oh, no. I married you lifetimes before that: when I was twelve and stood in front of the bathroom mirror and wrote our names in fog; when I was thirteen and you were coming to my house to take me to the movies on a rainy Saturday afternoon, and I stood on the tips of my toes looking out the window for you, my feet all scrunched up in those impossible Mary Janes.

VICTOR: I can't be that young boy for you, anymore. He's not there, he—

SHEILA: You could . . . you could be anyone you wanted to be if—

VICTOR: No! He doesn't exist anymore. It's like the pencil I had at Phan Rang or Da Linh that answered your letters . . . it got smaller and smaller trying to tell you what was happening, until there was nothing left of it but a little nub that had no words left in it at all.

The sounds of Captain Nakamochi's lovemaking begin again through the ventilation shaft, very softly at first.

I know you'd like to blame everything that's happened to us on Max, but he's never been the one to blame.

SHEILA: That's why we're two hundred miles out on the ocean with a propeller shaft that's probably held on by staples and oriental gumballs.

VICTOR: I don't want to listen to this.

SHEILA: He's crazy, you know. As crazy as everything that's happened to us since we met them. If I hadn't gotten hungry and made you pull off the freeway at that taco stand, all of this would have been just a nightmare. We never would have met her with her thirteen shades of eyeliner and her thirty-six-inch perfect tits; we never would have met him, orating over a cheese burito with the sauce dripping into his moustache. We would have gone back to New York. You would have taken that job—

As they begin a squall of an argument, their words clash against each other, interrupting, overlapping.

VICTOR: No! No! I never would have taken that job, never gone back!

SHEILA: We would now be a family with a sky's-the-limit future, instead of a pair of clowns—

VICTOR: Because once I got off that plane, I had no place to go! There was no address left in me!

SHEILA:—following around a man with yellowed-up accounts of a mine disaster he caused, crumbling away in his pocket!

VICTOR: I want you to get off his back about what happened in that mine! He was exonerated!

SHEILA: Tell that to the thirteen men who didn't make it out!

A new element has been added to Captain Nakamochi's increasingly intrusive lovemaking—a scratchy phonograph needle being irritatingly jarred along the grooves of a record, Puccini's La Bohème.

VICTOR (*Exploding*): What is that? What the hell is that?

SHEILA: It's nothing. It's Nakamochi.

VICTOR: It's *La Bohème*! He's playing *La Bohème* while he's getting screwed!

SHEILA (*Trying to keep her husband focused on the argument she feels she must make*): Forget about him. He's not important.

Victor just keeps staring at the vent.

Victor? What do we do if it gets worse and worse for us?

VICTOR: It's over with.

SHEILA: Only this time is over with. What happens the next time? Suppose the next business doesn't work out the way we want it to? Do we torch that one, too? And if somebody gets in our way, what do we do then?

VICTOR (*Shouting into the vent*): Will you hold it down in there?

SHEILA: Arrange a little accident? A shove in the river? A ride in a car that doesn't have any brakes?

VICTOR: You're taking crazy.

SHEILA: Am I? How much of a step is it from arson to that? You see, I can't even say the word. I say "that." Is it a giant step? A tiny little step? Or do we just turn around one day and it's done? I love you; I always have and I always will. You were the only boy who made me feel I could be pretty, loved me even when I knew I had all the charm and personality of a toad; but now, standing here with you, I have the feeling that everything in our life is hanging so delicately between farce and destruction I don't even want to breathe. I'm afraid of one little breath one way or the other.

VICTOR: You're letting this get all blown up in your mind out of proportion.

SHEILA: Am I? He's taken everything away from you. Your intelligence, your talent.

VICTOR (*Running over to the vent*): I want you to hold it down in there! You hear me?

SHEILA: You've gone from a man who was going to do wonderful things with his life to an arsonist who trips over his own candles.

What were you trying to do in that warehouse, Victor? Burn yourself to death?

VICTOR (*Totally losing control over the disturbance coming from the vent*): I said that's enough! (*Jumping up, smashing his hand against the vent*) Shut up! Shut up in there! I can't hear myself think!

Suddenly there is a bang, and the ship begins shuddering, vibrating again.

What the hell is going on with this fucking ship?

Outside the lounge, pandemonium has broken out: men yelling in a polyglot of languages, footsteps running. Victor flings open the door to the deck, grabbing Captain Nakamochi who is just racing by, naked except for his hat and shorts.

What the hell is going on here? What's wrong with this ship?

CAPTAIN: Propeller shaft breaking! Everything breaking! (*Angrily wrenching his arm free*) You do this! You and your friend do this!

Racing away, Victor shouting after.

VICTOR: We didn't do anything! You were the one who said this ship was in excellent condition!

There is a final bang as the ship's engine cuts out in abrupt finality. Victor turns from the door to Sheila.

He was the one who said this ship was in excellent condition.

The last few notes of the duet between Mimi and Rodolfo ending Act I of La Bohème *die away, as the lights fade and out.*

END OF ACT ONE

ACT TWO

Scene 1

The ship's deck. That afternoon.

A brilliant sun illuminates the deck, casting a clear line of light and shadow. The deck is cluttered with assorted marine equipment: canvas, rope, wooden cargo platforms.

Annie, in shorts and high-heeled shoes, is stretched out on a chaise lounge she has carried up from the cabin. She is directly in the sun and seems as comfortable as if she were on vacation in some resort. Her sunglasses rest momentarily on top of her head, and a plastic drawstring bag lies by the side of the chair next to her purse. For some moments she applies suntan lotion to her body, and then there is the sound of someone noisily climbing up the stairwell to the deck, banging metal on metal, step after step after step. Sheila enters, her fur coat tucked under her arm, a straight-back aluminum chair trailing behind. She is dressed even more frumpily than usual, an outfit complete with her crepe-soled walking shoes. Although her hair is still wet from a recent shower, she appears hot, sweaty and uncomfortable. She stops for a moment as she enters, catching her breath, surveying the deck and the broiling sun above it.

SHEILA: Oh, God. (*As she sufferingly makes her way toward Annie, dragging her chair along the deck, her shoes stick to the deck with every sticky step*) How can it be so hot? So hot, so filthy. Oil over everything. Rust. Grease. Tar.

Setting herself up near Annie, but safely in the shade. Annie, seeing how uncomfortable she is with the fur coat on her lap, goes over to her.

ANNIE: Here, give me the coat.

SHEILA: What for?

ANNIE: I'll put it down someplace.

SHEILA (*Truly shocked*): You can't put it down here! You have any idea what tar does to sealskin? It ruins it. You can't get it off.

ANNIE: I'm not going to get any tar on it, and even if I did you most certainly can take it off.

SHEILA: No, you can't. When those seal things are alive, it comes off.

They swim around in all that disgusting oily shit off the California coast, and it comes right off. But once they're dead, it won't come off anymore.

ANNIE: That's ridiculous.

SHEILA: They must lick it off. They must have some kind of natural dissolving agent in their tongue.

ANNIE (*Giving up and returning to her chair*): You should have left it in the cabin.

SHEILA: Why? So it'll get stolen? You have any idea what this coat is worth?

ANNIE: You can't keep lugging it around wherever you go.

SHEILA: This is a four-thousand-dollar coat. It's as good as cash. All I'd have to do is put an ad in the paper and I could sell it anywhere.

Looking at Annie comfortably stretched out in the sun, applying her lotion.

How can you sit in the sun that way? Don't you know what the sun does to the skin? It makes it all wrinkled and ugly.

ANNIE: You know I like the sun. I always sit in the sun.

SHEILA: You sit in the sun at the beach. This is hot metal.

ANNIE: I'm not on hot metal. I'm sitting in a chair.

SHEILA: The heat radiates up. Don't you feel the heat waves radiating up from the deck?

ANNIE: Not particularly.

SHEILA: The whole deck is shimmering. This ship must look like a mirage in the Gobi desert. There's probably some Mongolian jock out there somewhere on his camel, staring at us right now, watching this ship go floating by.

As Annie finishes applying her suntan lotion.

You even brought suntan oil? Twenty minutes to pack before we left and you took suntan oil? What did you do, just empty out the medicine cabinet?

ANNIE: I didn't think about it. I went to grab the ointment for Max's hands and then I just swept everything in.

SHEILA: What other crap did you bring? I can see you got eyeliner on.

ANNIE: I don't know. The usual: lipstick, face powder, some of the Chanel No. 5 we had left over from Montevideo, my loofah sponge, the wig.

SHEILA: Junk. A total collection of valueless junk. With the exception of the Picasso print you didn't bring anything worth anything.

ANNIE (*Holding out the suntan lotion*): You want some?

SHEILA: Why would I want some more greasy mess on me? Look at the bottom of my shoes. (*Lifting up her foot*) There's tar all over them. (*Turning the shoe so she can look at it*) Tar all over the sole. (*Looking at the other sole*) Both of them. This ship is one gigantic dirtbag. I keep sticking to the deck. Every time I take a step it feels like I stepped into a wad of bubble gum. I can't stand it. Didn't you get tar on your shoes?

ANNIE: I don't know. I didn't notice.

SHEILA (*Staring at her for several moments, and then actually curious enough to make the effort to walk over into the sun and inspect the bottom of Annie's shoes*): You got more tar on them than mine!

ANNIE: Really? I didn't notice.

SHEILA: How can you not notice? You can't lift your foot without sending half your calf muscles into spasm. It feels like there's sticky vines growing up out of the deck gumming themselves around your ankles.

ANNIE: I guess the tar doesn't stick to the sole as much with leather as it does with crepe. We have different soles on our shoes. (*Pulling out another pair of shoes from her drawstring bag*) If you like, I'll lend you a pair of mine.

Holding them out to Sheila, who stares at them with open contempt.

SHEILA: I'm not going to walk around this ship in a pair of open-toed fuck-me shoes with six-inch stiletto heels! (*Returning to her chair*) You didn't pack a book or anything, did you?

ANNIE: No.

SHEILA: I was in the middle of reading *The Flounder* when we left. I had it by the end table by the door, and I kept reminding myself to take it, and then I forgot.

ANNIE (*Lifting her glasses and looking at Sheila*): What book was that you were reading?

SHEILA: *The Flounder.*

ANNIE: By who?

SHEILA: Gunter Grass.

ANNIE: Oh. (*Putting her glasses back on and stretching out again*)

SHEILA: "Oh," what? Did you read it?

ANNIE: No. I read part of *Moby Dick* in high school. I thought it might have been the same author, but it's not.

Sheila just stares at her for several moments in silence.

You ever read *Moby Dick*?

SHEILA (*Responding as if someone had asked a Talmudic scholar if he had ever glanced at the Bible*): Yes.

ANNIE: It's a good book. I liked it. I got up to the part about Queequeg.

SHEILA: That's the first twenty pages.

ANNIE: The way he described him with his purple-yellow face and that little idol thing he carried around in the bag. It was very interesting.

SHEILA (*Nodding her head up and down, listening to Annie's comments on* Moby Dick): I'm going to go crazy before this boat docks. I can feel my sanity slipping away from me. No books. No cigarettes. (*Rummaging in her purse until she pulls out a cigarette butt. Holding it up*) I found this on the stairwell. God knows what diseases those lips had that smoked this. (*Lighting up the butt*)

ANNIE: You can pick up all the books and cigarettes you want in Tamatave.

SHEILA: That's days from now.

ANNIE: That's not so long. You could borrow a magazine from somebody. There's magazines all over the ship.

SHEILA: Sex magazines.

ANNIE: They have articles in them.

SHEILA: What articles? "The Sailor's Guide to Getting Laid in Singapore"? You think that's my idea of reading material?

Pause, as she watches Annie slightly change her position on the lounge chair.

You know, if I were you, I wouldn't dress like that on this ship.

ANNIE: What's the matter with the way I'm dressed?

SHEILA: It's too provocative, unless you're purposely trying to excite those men. You ever wonder what it would be like if a horde of them just decided to come swarming up on deck and take us by force? Who'd stop them? This isn't civilization. We're not protected here. Men walk around safe all the time. Women are never any safer than the biggest scrotum sack allows them to be. That's why I'm dressed the way I am.

ANNIE (*Slowly taking a look at Sheila's frumpy outfit*): That's the way you always dress. Besides there's nobody around.

SHEILA: Don't kid yourself. They're all over this ship—half of them in their underwear with their pubic hairs and worse hanging out.

You can't take ten steps up a stairwell without feeling their eyeballs sliding up your legs like a radar scan. Why would you say I dress like this all the time?

ANNIE: You do.

SHEILA: I happen to have some very nice dresses. You've seen me in them.

ANNIE: They're all the same. They look like Hefty Bags.

SHEILA: Well, I don't make a point of dressing for men.

Pause, while she waits for a reply to her retort. There is none.

I dress for myself.

Another pause. Again there is no response.

You dress for men.

After some moments when her third retort has provoked no response, Sheila becomes aware that the sunlight is creeping up on her.

Why is the sun following me around? (*Looking at the pool of sunlight around her as if it were some malevolent thing*) I sat down in the shade not two minutes ago and now it's all over me!

ANNIE: The ship is turning.

SHEILA: (*Standing up, alarmed*): You mean we're just drifting? We're not attached to anything? Aren't they supposed to put out an anchor, or something?

ANNIE: It's too deep. It's thousands of feet down.

SHEILA: Then what good is it having an anchor? If you can't use it when you need it, what's the purpose in having it? (*Pulling her chair further into the shade*) I'm not going to have any shade to rely on. I'm just going to have to keep moving my chair around and around!

ANNIE: We're not going around and around. The boat is just rocking back and forth a little in the current.

SHEILA (*Looking over the side of the ship*): There isn't any current out there. The water's like glass. Filthy green glass with chunks of garbage and those blue jellyfish bladders floating through it with their tentacles. Is that garbage ours? Are they following the ship feeding on our garbage, or what?

ANNIE: Why don't you go down to the cabin and relax, Sheila? Take another shower. Max got them to pipe in nice fresh water. You got a fan. It's nice and cool.

SHEILA: It's not nice and cool! It's hot! It's hot with the fan! It's hot with the shower! That's why I came up on deck! (*Staring wildly about her*) I've got no place to go! Even if I sit in the shade the sun starts coming after me!

ANNIE: We'll be on our way soon. Just as soon as they fix the propeller shaft.

SHEILA: Suppose they can't fix it? They've been trying to fix that damn thing since this morning, and we're still sitting here.

ANNIE (*Going over to her, concerned by Sheila's distress*): They'll fix it. Come on now, why don't you sit down here in the shade? We'll be on our way before you know it.

SHEILA (*Not moving*): You don't know that! (*Looking out at the ocean again*) It's just like the *Ancient Mariner*. No wind. No movement.

ANNIE: We don't need any wind. This isn't a sailboat, Sheila. We've got an engine. We've got a radio. Worse comes to worse we can always call for a tow.

SHEILA: Listen to me! We're not stuck with a flat on the L.A. freeway, waiting for the three A's! We're out in the middle of the ocean! (*Staring at the ocean again*) My God, that's probably what the Ancient Mariner said after they shot the albatross: "Worse comes to worse we can always get a tow."

ANNIE: I doubt if he ever said anything like that. Now, come on, let's just sit down.

SHEILA (*Allowing herself to be escorted back*): How would you remember him saying anything? You never read past the first twenty pages of anything! If they were going to fix that damn propeller thing, they would have gotten it fixed by now.

ANNIE: They will get it fixed. Max and Victor are with them now.

SHEILA: What does that have to do with anything?

ANNIE: They're trying to help Captain Nakamochi repair the ship.

SHEILA: We're two hundred miles out in the ocean, drifting around in a dead sea filled with garbage and those things in the garbage, and that Japanese moron is relying on Max and Victor?

Annie stretches out on her lounge chair again.

What is the matter with you? Neither of them knows anything about ship's engines. Max has both his hands in bandages and Victor hasn't been able to open up a can of tennis balls in the last fifteen years without collecting major medical insurance!

ANNIE: Why do you always do that? Make everything seem worse than it is?

SHEILA: I'm not making anything seem worse than it is. It is worse than it is!

ANNIE: As a matter of fact, Max says his fingers are feeling much better and he may even take the bandages off by tomorrow; and as for your husband, it seems to me he commanded an infantry company in the war and went from second lieutenant to captain in less than two years, so I hardly think he needs major medical insurance to open up a can of tennis balls.

SHEILA: That was then, this is now; and you don't have to defend my husband to me. I'm not the one who ragged him about the Shahistan rug purchase, or have you forgotten about that?

ANNIE: No, I haven't, and I was wrong. There were lots of purchases he made and they were very good ones. I was just a little upset because you seemed to want to blame Max for everything. I've already cleared all that up with him before he went down to fix the engine.

SHEILA: Oh, really?

ANNIE: Yes. Max reminded me how capable a chemist Victor really is, and I've cleared that up.

SHEILA: Well, that's wonderful. Too bad that engine isn't a test tube.

ANNIE: It doesn't matter. They're going to repair it.

SHEILA: They can't repair it! My husband doesn't know anything about ships, and Max's hands are still burnt no matter how good his fingers are feeling!

ANNIE: It doesn't matter! The drive shaft to the propeller will be repaired, and they will repair it!

Rising up in a face-to-face confrontation with Sheila. For some long moments they glare at each other, and then the ship's engine starts up with a loud whir that mounts and mounts in smooth operational intensity. A slow smile of satisfaction spreads across Annie's lips as she lies back down in apparent triumph. For some moments more the smooth sound of the engine is heard and then there is a heavy bang, followed by a sickening vibration and silence. The smile drains from Annie's face.

SHEILA (*Sitting down*): The sound of the world: a bunch of men fucking over their Tonka toys, pretending they know what they're doing. I keep getting this image of us sitting here like the Ancient Mariner while the ship drifts off into the Antarctic.

ANNIE: Did you ever actually see an albatross, Sheila?

SHEILA: No.

ANNIE: It's a big stupid-looking bird with a nose like a tube. Mr. Conroy, our nature-study teacher, brought in a stuffed one when we were reading the poem. Once a week on Friday afternoon they took us into the nature-study room. Everything was stuffed: a stuffed raven, a stuffed passenger pigeon, a stuffed albatross. They even had a stuffed mandrill head. We were supposed to wander around the room, studying them.

SHEILA: I wonder how long it would take to get another ship out here to rescue us?

ANNIE: They fired Mr. Conroy for rubbing up against the girls. You'd be standing there looking at the mandrill and he'd rub against you.

SHEILA: That is disgusting.

ANNIE: He didn't bother you if you stood by the birds. It was just by the mandrill.

SHEILA: Is that supposed to make it any less disgusting? What grade was this?

ANNIE: Seventh.

SHEILA: Oh, that is really disgusting.

ANNIE: He was just a little man who'd lost his wife. They said he didn't do anything like that before she passed away.

SHEILA: I wouldn't let a man like that get within ten feet of me.

ANNIE: Then you didn't stand by the mandrill . . . look at its pointed beard . . . the blue-and-scarlet ribbing of its muzzle.

SHEILA: That what you did?

ANNIE: He wasn't any different than any of the other boys who thought a fifty-cent movie ticket and a box of popcorn entitled them to tear me apart in their car. He was just the first. (*Her voice seems almost coming from a reverie, gradually entered into*) Dirty little town with its dirty little mines and mills, and its dirty little houses all rowed up on top of each other like nothing was meant to breathe. Every spring my mother kept trying to grow something in that dead soil in front of our house—caladium, primrose, verbena—nothing came up except it was leafless or stunted. And the boys stupid as I was stupid . . . going nowhere, knowing nothing, disappearing into the mills right after high school if they waited that long . . . never coming home except being drunk . . . loudmouthed and sour as their fathers with a bellyful of anger and a fist. And then one day my father brought home a young man from the Windber mine. His hands were clean, and he wore a tie, and you didn't have to talk to him two minutes to see how very uncommon he was, how much he believed in things and cared . . . not someone you'd ever roll away from in bed in the middle of the night feeling betrayed. Sitting there at the table, he seemed to me everything I was reaching for all my life, and when he looked at me I lowered my eyes, but my soul seemed to fall off-balance and trip.

SHEILA (*After some moments of silence, going over to her*): Are you awake?

ANNIE: Yes.

SHEILA: I think we ought to go down to the engine room and see what they're doing.

ANNIE: You go. I don't want to move right now.

SHEILA: I can't go down alone. I don't know my way around this ship.

ANNIE: There's nothing to know. You just keep going down.

SHEILA: Into what? The crew quarters? Open up one of those bulkhead things by mistake and end up in a roomful of animals, smoking hashish and drooling over their lunch?

ANNIE: Then stay here. The ship will be on its way in a little while.

SHEILA: No, it won't. Faith is a wonderful thing, Annie, except when it's misplaced. Then it isn't a virtue anymore.

ANNIE: I don't think real faith is ever misplaced, Sheila.

SHEILA: When it gets misplaced, it becomes a vice. Maybe they would like to fix it, but just can't.

ANNIE (*Sitting up, taking off her glasses, looking directly at Sheila, and speaking in a voice filled with intensely controlled anger*): But that isn't what Max said to me, Sheila. What he said was that he was going to go down there and fix it! He and Victor were going to go down there and fix it! Now what that means to me, Sheila, is that they will fix it! The drive shaft to that propeller will be fixed!

She continues to stare at Sheila as the engine abruptly cuts in, whirs for a time in smooth operation before giving way to a bang, a sickening vibration that cuts out into silence exactly as before.

There!

SHEILA: "There," what?

ANNIE: The change in the propeller sound.

SHEILA: I didn't hear any change in the propeller sound.

ANNIE: From what it was a few minutes ago.

SHEILA: Yes, that's right. From what it was a few minutes ago.

Waiting for a reply from Annie that doesn't come.

The same whirring sound. The same vibration.

Again waiting for a reply from an Annie who just glares at her.

Even the bang was absolutely the same.

ANNIE: Why are you doing this?

SHEILA: Doing what?

ANNIE: Making yourself sound so much like Mary-Ellen Sawyer.

SHEILA: I don't know any Mary-Ellen Sawyer.

ANNIE: She used to live next door to me in Morrellville. She said my thighs were too thick to try out for the cheerleaders. All the time I was exercising and dieting, she kept pretending she couldn't see any change. Even when I won the Miss Johnstown contest and went on to Harrisburg, she was still pretending she couldn't see the change.

SHEILA: I don't think I'm doing that.

ANNIE: You know what happened to Mary-Ellen Sawyer? She ended up standing behind the costume jewelry counter of Friedman Brothers department store until she developed ugly varicose veins.

The engine starts up a third time with the exact same success and failure as before. For some moments Annie remains motionless in the silence and then she gathers up her belongings.

I thought it sounded much better that time.

Annie exits, head up, high heels clicking.

SHEILA (*Shouting after, as much for her benefit as Annie's*): Well, you just don't want to know what's true!

Lights fade and out.

Scene 2

The deck. That evening.

Max stands by the ship's railing, the ends of his oil-stained bandages beginning to unravel. He has a small yellowed newspaper article in his hand and he stares at it. After some moments, he hears the sound of footsteps approaching, an argument in progress, and he folds the article back into its well-worn creases, and closes his hand about it. Captain Nakamochi enters with Victor right on his heels. Neither man sees Max.

VICTOR: Hold it a minute! Will you just hold it a minute? All I want to do is just talk to you.

CAPTAIN: I don't listen to you anymore! Wrong to leave Cape Town with a bad propeller shaft! Wrong to let your friend try to fix it and not call for tow!

VICTOR: Then let's forget about trying to fix it. All I'm asking is that you get the ship towed to another port. If they can't take us to Tamatave—

CAPTAIN: Tam'atave too far!

VICTOR: I know that. All I want you to do is take us to another port. Just not Cape Town.

CAPTAIN: Not possible! No repair place for me anywhere else.

VICTOR: We cannot go back to Cape Town. You know that.

CAPTAIN: I know nothing!

VICTOR: Don't hand me that! You took our money, and you know perfectly well we can't go back to Cape Town! Now how much more do you want? We'll pay whatever you want!

CAPTAIN: No! No more paying me to do wrong things! (*Pulling the envelope full of money that Annie had given him out of his pocket, and thrusting it in Victor's hands*) You take back your money! I don't know how you got on this ship. You sneak on ship. No one see you.

VICTOR (*Angrily grabbing Captain Nakamochi by the collar*): Listen to me, you son of a bitch! You tow us back to Cape Town and I'll tell them you were in on that fire with us right from the beginning! I'll tell them you helped us escape for money! Then we'll see what happens to your license and this filthy ship of yours!

CAPTAIN: I don't care what you do! I don't listen to you or your friend, anymore! Your friend too clever with words! He gets me to do a bad thing! (*Struggling to free himself, but Victor is too strong*)

MAX: Let him go, Vic.

For a moment, Victor holds onto the struggling captain, and then he thrusts him away.

CAPTAIN (*To Max, as he exits*): No more listening to you! No more wrong things!

VICTOR (*Shouting after him*): He didn't make you do anything you didn't want to, you greedy bastard! If that propeller shaft was in such bad condition, it was your fault! You should have had it taken care of a long time ago!

For a few moments Victor stands there trying to catch his breath, and then he walks over to Max. Captain Nakamochi comes running back in to get the last word.

CAPTAIN: You want to eat? Everything now à la carte! Triple, triple extra! (*Hastening back off before Victor has a chance to come after him*)

VICTOR (*Joining Max at the railing*): I cannot believe this fucking bad luck we've been having! First the candle falls over into the gasoline; then the propeller shaft falls apart as fast as you put it together; and now the only tow we can get is back to Cape Town? This is turning out to be the worst goddamn disaster since Sheila decided to write her own marriage vows! What the hell is wrong with that propeller shaft, anyway?

MAX: Metal fatigue. It should have been replaced a long time ago.

VICTOR: Then why didn't that son of a bitch do it? That's his job, isn't it? That's why they made him captain of this fucking ship!

MAX: I guess not everybody does his job.

VICTOR (*Noticing the article in Max's hand*): Why don't you get rid of that? Just open up your hand and let it blow away.

MAX: Why? You think that's going to make me forget? You forget about that woman who hit your car with that sign?

VICTOR: At least you wouldn't have something to keep reminding you of it.

MAX (*Striking his temples with his fingers*): This is what reminds me of it. This! (*Holding out the article for a moment before he puts it away*) *This* is just a list of names stuffed in a wallet. I used to think I was going to do something for them, but once you're dead, who's gonna do anything for you, right? Then I thought I could do something for that roomful of women sitting in back of me at the hearing, waiting and waiting for justice in their worn-out cotton dresses from Woolworth. But I couldn't do anything for them, either—no matter what kind of fantasies I had about getting rich and paying them off for their sons and husbands. It was just not going to be sufficient to come back and kick over their tubs of filthy laundry and buy them washing machines! Just not sufficient recompense!

VICTOR: Sometimes you have to accept just being acquitted, Max. You start thinking about what you do in this world, you end up going down on all fours howling at the moon.

MAX: I wasn't acquitted! They just didn't find me criminally negligent. I told you that.

VICTOR: All right. The same thing. You walk, you walk.

MAX: It's not the same thing to me.

VICTOR: Everybody fucks up, Max. If not here, then tomorrow; if not now, then yesterday. That's the drill. The only thing anybody owes this world is indifference.

MAX: Yeah? Well, maybe it's not good enough for me—fucking up! Not good enough to have a responsibility not to *fuck up*, and *fuck up*! I don't give a shit about not being found criminally negligent! I don't give a shit about any of those self-serving excuses those legal geniuses found for me—the boy is only twenty-two; it's only the second mine he's inspected! I knew how to do my job. I just didn't do it! I let those bastard mine owners walk me right through the mine, flattering me with their attention, puffing me up like one of their good old boys with their arms around me, their cigars and jokes, while right over my head the rock strata is fractured! Those greedy bastards with their greedy machines grubbing out every last inch of profit had fractured the rock strata, and walked me right by it! I thought I was looking! I thought I was seeing! Eight hours later, while I'm having a steak dinner in Wheeling, bones are being broken, bodies are being buried, and I still think *I am looking*! Still think *I am seeing*!

VICTOR: Let me fix your bandages, Max. They're coming all unraveled.

MAX: Never gonna be good enough for me to have a sworn duty to do something, and not do it! Never!

Noticing that Victor is reaching for his bandages.

They're fine.

VICTOR: How can they be fine? Come on.

MAX: They're fine! By tomorrow I'm going to take all these bandages off. There's no point babying something that doesn't have to be babied. (*Walking away a few feet*) Before the propeller shaft broke down that final time, I was ranging in on some new prospects for our business in Tasmania. Something we could get under way even with the little money we have left.

VICTOR: That's great, Max.

MAX: It's easy enough to start up a new business when you've got plenty of capital. The trick is to do it when what you've got left is next-to-nothing, and it absolutely has to be protected.

VICTOR: You got any idea what we're going to do about that tow vessel Nakamochi called? I figure it's going to get out here a lot quicker than we did. (*Expecting an answer, but there is none*) So that gives us less than twelve hours to figure out what we're going to do. (*Again, no answer*) Once we're under tow it's going to be too late.

MAX: I don't know what to do about that tow ship, Vic.

VICTOR: So we'll think about it like we always do. If you want I could give it one more shot with Nakamochi, but I don't think it'd do any good. The son of a bitch is determined to go back to Cape Town.

MAX: He doesn't have any other choice.

VICTOR: Yeah. So the next thing I was thinking about was that when that tow ship gets here we switch over to it. You know, hide out somewhere on it.

MAX: They'll search the tow ship right after they get done searching this one . . . if Nakamochi just doesn't give us up outright.

VICTOR: So . . . so that's not going to work, either. So we keep thinking . . . always an option, right?

MAX: Sometimes you run out of options: candles get knocked over; boats go dead in the water.

VICTOR: A bunch of lousy accidents, that's all.

MAX: Are they, Vic? Did it ever occur to you that all these accidents ruining everything we've tried to do all these years might not be accidents at all? That somewhere out there was an Intelligence playing a game against us, and we don't even know the rules?

VICTOR: I don't really believe in things like that, Max.

MAX: We're like the yokel at the country fair who enters the gypsy's tent thinking he can play the game and win. We're young. The vision we have of things in front of us is so clear it seems reflected off diamonds, and life's no cheap carnival of tricks . . . until the tent flap shuts . . . until the light fades and we're trapped in a game played without light at all! Pieces move in the dark, crashing down . . . everything above our head crashing down, thick, heavy, weight upon weight crushing until every breath is pain . . . until it's just easier to stop . . . breathing.

VICTOR: Is that what you're going to do, Max? (*Suddenly grasping Max by the shoulders and turning him around*) Look at me! Is that what you're gonna do, because there isn't anybody else! There's you, and there's me, and there's Annie, and there's Sheila, and that's all our world's come down to. All that's left after everything else that was us got lost. I don't know what any of us once was, or started out to be, but I do know that sometimes when things get broken into a lot of different pieces, you can take all the broken parts and reassemble them into something else. Maybe it can't do what it used to, but it can still do something. Who says a butterfly can only fly with the wings of a butterfly? Maybe, if it has to, it can fly with the wings of a bumblebee! Maybe, if it has to, it can walk with the legs of a fly! It's worth a try. You know what I say, Max? We play the game out, and the hell with the way the four of us look together when we cross the finish line!

MAX (*After a long pause*): There's one way. If Nakamochi can radio for a tow, maybe we can use that same radio to find another ship.

VICTOR (*As the idea sinks in*): You're right. He's got a radio. You're absolutely right! (*Pacing around the deck in a state of mounting excitement*) We're in the shipping lanes! There must be other freighters out here, maybe even a small passenger ship! (*Excitedly grabbing Max*) It's going to work! It's really going to work! (*Continuing his pacing*) And we've got the money to make it worth their while to go out of their way a little bit to pick us up! The son of a bitch was so anxious to wash his hands of us he gave us back practically everything we paid him!

MAX: Yes, we have the money.

VICTOR (*Grabbing Max again*): You did it, Max! You did it! You're always so worried about letting other people down, but you don't! You never let us down!

MAX: I don't want to let anyone down again, Vic.

VICTOR: And you don't, man! You're always there for us! You always come through! You see?

Victor's infectious joy catches hold in Max, and a small smile begins to light his face.

MAX: Why don't you go on up there and give it a try, Vic? Go on.

VICTOR: By myself?

MAX: Sure. Why not?

VICTOR (*Hesitant*): I thought the both of us would go up there. You know you can talk anybody into anything. I get one of those ship captains on the horn and some problem comes up, it's liable to go down sour.

MAX: No, it won't. You can do it. It's important for you to do it. Now, go on, before that tow vessel gets here and we all get dragged back to Cape Town.

VICTOR (*Looking at Max for some moments, weighing it all over in his mind, balancing his courage with his hidden fears, until he comes to a decision*): Okay. Okay!

Starting to exit on the run, excitedly, as Sheila and Annie enter, Sheila wearing her fur coat. He brushes by them, stops, turns to Max.

Wish me luck.

MAX (*Raising his bandaged thumb in the air*): You got it, buddy.

Victor exits.

SHEILA: Luck for what? (*Shouting after Victor*) Where are you going? What did he talk you into doing?

VICTOR (*Offstage; shouting back*): He'll tell you!

SHEILA: Tell me what? (*But this time there is no answer to her shout. She goes over to Max*) Tell me what?

MAX: Sit down for a moment, both of you. I do want to say something.

SHEILA: Here it comes. The propeller fell off and sank in five thousand fathoms.

MAX: Not quite.

SHEILA: Victor is putting on his snorkel gear and getting set to do underwater repairs on that fucking propeller shaft!

ANNIE: What's wrong, Max?

SHEILA: Notice please the question: "What's wrong?" Never what's right. In the natural course of human events everyone is entitled to ask at least once, "What's right?" It's guaranteed in the Constitution. Why does this not happen to us? Why are we not getting what we are entitled to? (*Shouting to the heavens*) Why is all happiness forbidden to Sheila?

ANNIE: Will you please be still? What is it, Max?

MAX: The propeller shaft can't be repaired.

SHEILA: Of course not. If it could be repaired it would be four other people on another boat.

MAX: The entire shaft has to be replaced and that means this ship is going to have to be towed in. Captain Nakamochi has already called in for one of this line's tow vessels.

SHEILA: Towed in where? Borneo? East Jesus? Don't you just love it?

MAX: Well, that's the thing. We're too far from Tamatave to be towed there, and this ship's line doesn't have any repair facilities at either Port Elizabeth or Durban.

SHEILA: When you say "line," Max, just so I understand you, are you implying that there are actually more ships like this floating around out there? That somebody has actually had the consummate balls to assemble an entire armada of these rotting corroded hulks and is busily turning a profit on them?

ANNIE: Where are they going to tow the ship, Max?

MAX: Well . . . like I said, that's the thing.

SHEILA: What thing? What thing are you talking about? (*When Max doesn't answer right away*) Oh, my God! We're going to be towed back to Cape Town!

ANNIE: Max?

SHEILA: It's Cape Town! You can see it in his eyes!

MAX: She's right, Annie. Captain Nakamochi doesn't have any other alternative, as far as this ship is concerned. However—

SHEILA: It's the end! The coup de grace! When we were watching those stupid bullfights in Mexico I had a premonition. I knew we'd end up dead on the ground with red flags sticking out of our back.

ANNIE: We're going to be arrested if we return to Cape Town, Max.

SHEILA: Cape Town is not acceptable, Max! Cape Town is not viable, Max! Cape Town is five years in prison, wearing gray pajamas and . . . (*Holding up one of Annie's hands*) no nail polish!

MAX: I didn't say there weren't other possibilities for us. I just said this ship had no alternative but to return to Cape Town.

SHEILA: What does that mean? (*Turning to Annie*) Do you know what the Wise One has just said, because I don't.

MAX: It only means we can't stay with this ship. Therefore, Victor and I have come up with what I think is an excellent idea.

SHEILA: Here it comes. The zinger. The big doody-head idea wrapped up in a hundred layers of toilet paper so you forget what the hell's inside and think it's the Hope diamond.

MAX: Victor is going to radio whatever vessels are nearby to see if he can get them to take us on as passengers. And since Captain Nakamochi has felt it expedient to return almost all the money we gave him as an advance, I think we can safely afford to pay whatever fare they ask.

ANNIE: You think that's a real possibility, Max, someone coming to pick us up?

MAX: If there are other ships around. Yes.

ANNIE: That's wonderful, then! Isn't that wonderful, Sheila?

SHEILA: The Wise One has yet to tell us why Captain Nakamochi felt it so expedient to return our money.

MAX: I believe at the time he was under the mistaken assumption that we had no option but to return with him to Cape Town, and like most prudent men he was simply taking the precaution of protecting himself with a plausible alibi in the event of our arrest—a precaution that has unexpectedly doubled the money available to facilitate our escape. I now have every reason to believe our permanent freedom is almost a real possibility.

ANNIE: Of course it's a real possibility! Why shouldn't it be? With the money we have in the bandages and the money we got back from Captain Nakamochi we have almost seven thousand dollars! And if we need more her coat is worth four thousand, so all in all we could have eleven thousand dollars if we have to!

SHEILA: What does my coat have to do with any of this? I'm not selling my coat!

ANNIE: I didn't say you have to sell your coat. I just said it could be part of our assets, if we needed it.

SHEILA: You really have some nerve, you know that? You come on this ship with nothing but a wig box and a Gucci purse, and you start coming after me because I had the foresight to take things that have value. If we have to sell anything, we can take that Picasso of yours and make it part of our assets.

ANNIE: It's only a print. It's worthless.

SHEILA: Don't make me laugh. Ha. Ha. There's no such thing as a worthless Picasso print. Some of those lithographs are worth thousands and thousands of dollars.

ANNIE: Not when you buy them in a bookstore for nineteen dollars and ninety-five cents.

MAX: I think we ought to get back to—

Both women are far too caught up in their argument to pay Max any attention.

SHEILA: If it was a worthless print, why did you hang it in your dining room like it was the Mona Lisa, and let me gush over it every time I was there?

ANNIE: I never said it was real.

SHEILA: You never said it was phony, either!

ANNIE: What was I supposed to do?

MAX: Annie, come on . . .

ANNIE: Walk you around my home, saying, "This is phony. This is real. This is phony. This is real"? I assumed with your education you could tell the difference between the real thing and a fake!

SHEILA: Is that why you took it on this ship?

ANNIE: I took it on this ship because I like it whether it's real or not. I don't need real things because I can enjoy the copy!

SHEILA: You took it on this ship because you knew I thought it was real, and you wanted to continue the charade! You knew I would know it was a phony if you left it at home!

ANNIE: If I wanted you to believe it was real, why would I tell you it was a phony just now, for heaven's sake?

SHEILA: So you could get me to sell my coat! You've been after this coat ever since I put some money aside and bought it in Montevideo! You just can't stand the idea that I might have something that you don't have!

ANNIE: I don't want your coat! I don't even eat meat. I happen to be a vegetarian as you well know, so why on earth would I want the skins of dead animals hanging all over me?

SHEILA: There are plenty of vegetarians who walk around with fur coats! Thousands of them! Millions!

ANNIE: I wouldn't put those slimy seals on my back to save my life!

SHEILA: You didn't think they were so slimy this afternoon when you couldn't wait to get your hands on them! Well, this coat is mine! It's not group property! I paid for it and it's mine!

MAX: Nobody's asking you to give up your coat, Sheila.

SHEILA (*Flipping the coat shut tight about her, as she advances on Max*): That's right! This coat will not be sacrificed! Now you just figure out a way to make everything else right here, because going back to Cape Town is not viable!

MAX: That's what Victor is trying to do right now, Sheila.

SHEILA: Well, it's not going to work.

ANNIE: How do you know it's not going to work? It hasn't even been tried yet.

SHEILA: Because nothing ever works! Maybe if the Big Persuader had gone up there with him, he might have convinced some half-crazed cannibal in a war canoe to pick us up, but he didn't do that!

MAX: I thought it best for Victor's sake that he do this on his own.

SHEILA: Victor hasn't done anything on his own since he met you! So now you come up with another plan because you're the one who's made himself self-elected leader of the pack! I don't even know how to think anymore. I can't remember the rhyme scheme of a Petrarchan sonnet, and I won the senior class prize for writing the best imitation of one. A,b,a,b? or a,b,b,a? (*Throwing her hands up*) I want to get off this moronic ship! I want to sit down to a table with a clean cloth on it! Clean silverware that doesn't have the remains of Captain Nakamochi's last meal congealed on the tines! (*Taking a candy bar out of her pocket, tearing off the wrapper, eating the candy*) And I want food. Real food! Lamb with potato and artichoke pancakes. Salmon mousse with cheese puffs. No more slimy things with suction cups that slide off the plate every time the ship rolls! (*Munching another bite*) That man is a pig! I would just like to know if he started on worse boats than this and has been working his way up, or whether he started on better boats and has just been working his way down! (*To Max*) And what have you come up with about our business in Tasmania? Not that we're ever going to get there, but you asked me to trust you.

MAX: As a matter of fact, I have been giving it some thought.

SHIELA: You know how long that seven thousand dollars is going to last with the price of everything these days? Two days in a hotel room and a kangaroo sandwich!

MAX: I haven't had time to work out all the details yet, of course, but it involves maintenance supply and industrial cleaning.

A long pause in which Sheila thinks and thinks some more.

SHEILA: What is maintenance supply and industrial cleaning, Max?

MAX: Cleaning up hotels, condominiums, retail stores, supermarkets—that sort of thing. We do it at night when most of the businesses are closed . . . ourselves at first, and then when the money starts coming in we hire people who are unemployed without high-paying job skills. The initial outlay is minimal, the risk to capital slight, and the profit potential could be unlimited.

SHEILA: Are you talking about physically cleaning floors? Physically getting down on our hands and knees and cleaning floors?

MAX: (*His enthusiasm beginning to take possession of him*): I'm talking about everything! Windows! Walls! I'm talking about washing, waxing, vacuuming! I'm talking about going into a retail store or supermarket after it closes and getting it put in absolutely first-class condition by the time the first customer comes in in the morning!

ANNIE: By ourselves?

MAX: Only at first, sweetheart. We start off small. Only those businesses we can handle on our own. And we do a good job. We do the best job they've ever had. You know the kind of people they have doing those things now. They don't care, because there isn't any incentive to care. They leave the place almost as dirty as they found it. But we care! We give whoever hires us a Class A job. And from that we get referrals, and that's when we start hiring crews to go out. And we supervise those crews, give them some profit-sharing incentive to make sure they do the same A-1 job we do. We never let the quality go down. Inside of six months, or a year at the most, we can run this business without ever touching a mop or a bucket by ourselves!

SHEILA: What a wonderful prospect to look forward to, Max. I could be the first Bennington graduate to actually scrub floors for a living.

MAX: It would only be for a few months.

SHEILA: You don't even know if they need that kind of business!

ANNIE: Of course they do! You can't go anywhere where things don't have to be cleaned. People walk into a store, they leave filth. Counters get smeared with fingerprints, ashes from cigarettes get ground into the carpet, mud gets tracked in when it rains!

MAX: Grime doesn't pay.

SHEILA: What did you say?

MAX: I said, "Grime doesn't pay." It could be the logo on the letterhead we send out soliciting accounts. "Mottram and Finkelberg—You need us because grime doesn't pay!" (*Looking at Sheila*) Well, what do you think?

SHEILA: Oh, pul . . . eeze!

ANNIE: I think it's a wonderful idea, considering the limited money we have.

SHEILA: You won't think it's so wonderful when those false nails of yours begin dropping off into the mop bucket!

ANNIE: (*Proudly holding out her hand*): They're not false . . . they're real!

SHEILA: Well, then that's just perfect, too, isn't it? (*Turning to Max*) And why is it always Mottram and Finkelberg?

MAX: It could be the other way around. It doesn't matter.

SHEILA: Mottram and Finkelberg in Cape Town. Mottram and Finkelberg in Montevideo. Mottram and Finkelberg in Panama City.

ANNIE: You used to say it wasn't euphonious saying Finkelberg and Mottram.

SHEILA: Well, I changed my mind. It's just as euphonious saying Finkelberg and Mottram. As a matter of fact, it's more euphon—

Sheila is stopped in mid-sentence by the entrance of Victor. Annie runs over to him, excitedly.

ANNIE: Victor, we have some wonderful news! Max has just come up with a very good suggestion for our new business.

VICTOR: (*Trying to muster up some instant enthusiasm*): Hey, that's great. Really great.

SHEILA: No ship, right? You called up and the last ship on the ocean just went down off French Guiana.

VICTOR: No. There is a ship. The *Kobe Moru*.

SHEILA: A passenger ship?

VICTOR: Not exactly. An oil tanker.

Both women have their hopes up, all things considered.

ANNIE: Well, that's not too bad. We could make do.

MAX: Can we take it?

VICTOR: It's going to Cape Town.

ANNIE: Oh.

VICTOR: I'm sorry, Annie. I did everything I could. There just weren't any other ships out there right now.

MAX: We know that, Vic.

Max and Annie join Victor upstage, staring out at the sea.

SHEILA: Well, of course it's going to Cape Town! Where else would it be going? There isn't any Norway left in the world! There isn't any Florida left in the world! China! Alaska! I want to know why everything in the world is descending on Cape Town!

For a long moment Sheila's rhetorical question hangs in the air, and then Victor turns around to face her.

VICTOR: Maybe there's a magnet there.

SHEILA: What?

VICTOR: (*Walking by Sheila to sit downstage on one of the cargo platforms*): I said maybe there's a magnet there sucking everything to it. One of those great big magnets they used to buy you from the five-and-dime when you were a kid . . . all red with the tips painted silver.

SHEILA: I'm sure I don't know why you're talking like this.

VICTOR: Those magnets had so much juice in them you could stick 'em under the nose of some rotten kid you didn't like and totally suck his whole face off!

SHEILA: Does anyone know why he's talking like this?

ANNIE: (*Turning around*): I think everything is going to Cape Town because Mary-Ellen Sawyer just moved to Cape Town and invited the whole world to her party. We just didn't get the invitation on time.

SHEILA: (*As Annie walks past her*): By tomorrow night they're going to have us in prison! Does anybody know what they do to people in those prisons?

ANNIE: (*Sitting down next to Victor on the cargo platform*): Mary-Ellen Sawyer's invitations to me never arrived on time even though she only lived next door. Annie Sullivan sends her regrets to Mary-Ellen Sawyer for not making it to her sixteenth birthday on time, but her invitation got lost in transit.

SHEILA: They hang you from the ceiling in chains! You want an extra slice of bread you have to fight a German shepherd for it!

MAX: (*Turning around and heading downstage*): I think there's a hole in the floor of the ocean at Cape Town and everything is just getting sucked down it.

SHEILA: Well, I can see nobody here is interested in reality.

She walks toward the upstage railing to stare out at the sea, as Max sits down next to his wife on the cargo platform.

MAX: Maybe it's not even a hole. Maybe it was just a tiny crack that never was much of anything until it opened up and became something because nobody saw it.

VICTOR: (*Turning to Max, understanding it's the mine he's talking about*): Maybe nobody could see it.

MAX: Maybe it wasn't there! Maybe when there was somebody there to see it, it wasn't there! And then when there was nobody there to see it, it was there! (*Pause, as the possible truth of what happened in the mine sinks in*) Oh, Lord.

SHEILA: (*Turning, walking downstage to join them on the cargo platform, squeezing in, fur coat and all, between Annie and Victor*): I can just imagine what Mary-Ellen Sawyer's parties looked like in Morrellville, Pennsylvania: sixteen debutantes with coal dust sticking to the shellac in their beehive hairdos, standing by the punchbowl waiting for their escorts to arrive in the back of a Ford pickup.

ANNIE: At least my friends don't write me letters saying, "Oh, Sheila, how fabby, fabby all this traveling is you're doing. You must join us at Lutece when you finally come to rest. And I do want you to meet my husband, Wendell. Wendell has just been appointed to the board of directors at Lincoln Center."

SHEILA: Your friends don't write you letters because it takes them all day to figure out how to write a coherent sentence because the only punctuation they ever learned how to use is a period! And why are you reading my letters?

ANNIE: If you don't want your letters read, don't leave them lying next to the silverware on the dining-room table when you invite people over for dinner! I thought they were napkins. I didn't have my contact lenses in.

SHEILA: You have contact lenses?

ANNIE: Yes.

SHEILA: Since when?

ANNIE: Montevideo. You got a fur coat. I went in and got contact lenses.

SHEILA: I didn't know you needed glasses. I thought your eyes were perfect.

ANNIE: They're not perfect. They were perfect up to Montevideo and then they were not perfect.

SHEILA: I'm sorry. I didn't know that.

ANNIE: It's no big deal.

SHEILA: I thought everything you had was perfect.

ANNIE: No. (*Noticing Sheila is sitting on her coat*) You're going to stain your coat.

SHEILA: What's the difference? They're only going to take it away from me in prison. (*Thinking about it for a few more seconds and then flipping up the back of the coat so she's no longer sitting on it*) I wonder what kind of food they serve in prison.

ANNIE: Probably like the food they served in my high school.

SHEILA: What was that?

ANNIE: Spaghetti with meatballs, codfish cakes, macaroni in Velveeta sauce, tapioca.

SHEILA: I can't eat that.

ANNIE: I liked the Velveeta. I would have gone back for seconds, but I was afraid everyone would laugh at me. They said the Velveeta made the macaroni stick to the back of your throat. If you went back for seconds, they stuck their fingers in their throat and made gagging sounds.

SHEILA: Oh, pul . . . eeze!

ANNIE: Why are you even asking me what kind of food they serve? I thought you knew everything about their prisons? They hang you from the ceiling! They make you fight German shepherds!

SHEILA: I made it up . . . I don't know what they do in prisons.

MAX: Some of the best novels were written in prison.

SHEILA (*Wearily laying her head down against Victor's shoulder*): Actually, I don't know anything at all. I just make a lot of noise.

VICTOR (*Putting his arm around her*): We've got to do something.

SHEILA: It's so tiring having to make decisions for yourself every minute of the day.

VICTOR: Max?

MAX: Whatever you think, Vic. I really don't feel like thinking anymore.

Kabuki music, a final time.

The upstage scrim, a deep blue night sky, rolls down silent and unseen behind them, unfurling a mobile of perfect little silver stars.

Kabuki music dies away.

VICTOR: Annie?

ANNIE: It's nice just sitting here. It's so black out there except for the stars, you'd think they took away the sky.

SHEILA: I'd like to hit the sky with a hammer and watch all the pieces tumble down. My life is such a mess. (*Idly tearing the wrapper off another candy bar*) It seems like forever I've been trying to put it back in order, but I don't know when the disorder started.

ANNIE: You'd never think in all that blackness there could be hidden a dazzling yellow sun tomorrow.

SHEILA (*Biting into the candy bar with a loud decisive snap*): God, I can't stand it when they cover toffy nut crunch with dark chocolate! It makes everything else you can do with your mouth seem like such a waste of time.

For some long moments there is nothing but Sheila's enraptured devouring of the candy bar, and each person's private reaction to it.

ANNIE (*Finally provoked enough to say something*): Where do you keep getting those candy bars from?

SHEILA: The rowboat. It's full of them.

For some more moments there is nothing but the sound of Sheila's chomping, but slowly the significance of what she has said dawns in the minds of the others. The pupils of their eyes begin moving furtively about, and then almost simultaneously three heads turn to stare at Sheila, who eats on obliviously.

MAX: Which rowboat, Sheila?

SHEILA: Any of them. They're all filled with food.

For a moment longer nobody moves, and then Max hops off the cargo platform, followed wordlessly by Annie and Victor. Sheila hardly notices what is happening until they have almost exited upstage left.

Where are you going?

They exit. Sheila idly walks after them as far as the upstage railing of the boat. She stops there, curiously watching them for some seconds.

What are you doing? The food is inside the boat. All you have to do is stick your hand inside and . . .

Sound of the lifeboat winch being creakily turned, as the lifeboat is lowered to the water.

Oh, God!

The lifeboat splashes into the water. Sheila begins backing away as the three of them return.

VICTOR: Let's go.
SHEILA: Go where?
VICTOR: Into the lifeboat.
SHEILA: I don't want to go into the lifeboat.
ANNIE: It's right against the side of the ship.
SHEILA: That doesn't mean anything to me. What do I care if it's right against the side of the ship? You can't just float around the ocean in a lifeboat.
ANNIE: Of course you can. That's what they were designed for.
SHEILA: They were designed for when a ship sinks. This ship isn't sinking.
MAX: It's loaded with food, and by tomorrow or the next day another ship'll come along. It'll be okay.

Sheila continues to back away as they close in on her.

SHEILA: No, it won't. It's insane! The only reason we're jumping into that lifeboat is because you saw me eating a candy bar! (*Banging her head with her hands*) If I didn't eat the candy bar, we wouldn't be jumping into the lifeboat!
VICTOR: Come on, give me your hand. We'll jump together.
SHEILA: I don't want to jump together. I can't do it. I feel like a crazed billiard ball, bouncing off God knows what. It's insane!

VICTOR: (*Grabbing her about the waist and bodily carrying her over to the railing*): It's only twenty feet to the water. Come on. The boat's not going to stay against the side of the ship forever. Max is telling you the truth. By tomorrow or the next day another ship will come along. Everything is going to be okay.

SHEILA: No, it won't! All they got out there is garbage and those slimy electric things glowing in the dark with tentacles!

VICTOR: They won't hurt you. Nothing is going to hurt you.

SHEILA: You don't know that.

VICTOR: Will you trust me for once?

SHEILA: I'm finished! My life is over with! This is what it's come to! Yesterday was absurd; today is absurd; tomorrow's worse!

ANNIE: Stop being such a coward.

SHEILA: I want time to think. They gave Lady Jane Grey more time to think on the gallows. (*Desperately trying to find reasons to abort the jump*) I can't jump into the water with a four-thousand-dollar coat! It's going to be ruined.

VICTOR: It won't be ruined. It'll survive.

ANNIE: Which is more than what's going to happen to us if we don't get off this boat!

SHEILA: Everything's left in the cabin: the VCR, the Waterford lamp, our clothing! I've got to go down to the cabin and get it!

VICTOR: No time.

SHEILA: Of course there's time. Annie has to get her Picasso print.

ANNIE: It's a fake, remember? Now come on, let's go, Sheila. The spirit of God moved on the waters. It didn't say He stood still clawing onto the guardrail.

SHEILA: No sane person walks away and leaves a Waterford lamp behind!

VICTOR: (*Hoisting her over the railing*): Oh yes they do! Oh yes they do when they're on a ship where everything's à la carte and they need it to pay for the lifeboat! You wouldn't want us to leave this ship without paying Nakamochi for his lifeboat, would you? That would be an immoral unethical act.

SHEILA: Oh, God, it's as high as the Empire State Building! I can't do it!

VICTOR: You can do it. (*Joining her on the other side of the railing*) There's nothing to be afraid of. Just give me your hand.

SHEILA: That's easy for you to say. Your hand's attached to you, my hand's attached to me!

VICTOR: What the hell's that mean?

SHEILA: I don't know. I'm so frightened I don't know what I'm saying.

MAX: Would it help if Annie and I went first?

SHEILA: Yes! Yes! You and Annie go first!

ANNIE: I don't believe her. As soon as we jump, she's going to go running back to the cabin.

SHEILA: No. No. I'm not.

ANNIE: I can see it in her eyes. They look like a ferret's. She always gets that look when she's lying.

SHEILA: I'm going to jump! I'm going to jump!

As Annie and Max climb over the railing.

ANNIE: You don't jump after we do, I'm coming back with one of those tentacle things and I'm going to stick it down the back of your coat!

Max and Annie, hand in hand, leap into the water. Sound of their splash below; a spray of waterdrops plops on the deck.

VICTOR: Are you ready?

SHEILA: I'm scared.

VICTOR: I know you are. Just pretend it's the big sandbox at Van Cortlandt Park and we're jumping in.

SHEILA: That's ridiculous! The water is so dark, I can't even see them.

MAX and ANNIE (*Offstage*): We're here! We're here!

VICTOR: It's only dark till you jump into it. Once you're in the water it gets lighter.

SHEILA: That's even more ridiculous.

MAX and ANNIE (*Offstage*): Jump, Sheila! Jump!

SHEILA: Oh, God, they sound like those crazy people who are always telling suicides to jump.

ANNIE: (*Offstage*): The current's pulling us away!

VICTOR: We've got to go, now! I'm not going without you.

SHEILA: I can't do it! I keep thinking what's in there, what's out there!

VICTOR: No more thinking . . . (*Kissing her*) Just jump!

SHEILA: I love you.

VICTOR: I love you, too, even if you circled all the spelling errors in my love letters . . . now jump!

As the two of them, hand in hand, leap.

SHEILA: First the fire and now this! Ahhhhh!

The long scream of Sheila's fear trails after her until it is finally swallowed up by the sound of the splash far below. Again, waterdrops spray onto the deck.

SHEILA (*Offstage*): Oh, God, this water is alive!
VICTOR (*Offstage*): I know it is, so swim, Sheila! Swim for the lifeboat!
MAX and ANNIE (*Offstage*): We're here! We're here!
ANNIE (*Offstage*): Max has everything under control!
SHEILA (*Offstage; pause, followed by her cry*) Oh, God!

Lights dim and out.

END OF PLAY